Make Your Bed
Quilted Bed Runners, Pillows, and More to Suit Your Style

LESLEE EVANS

Martingale®
& COMPANY

Dedication

To my family

Those far away: Mom, Dad, Grandma Great, DaMarr, Gene, and my sisters, Lynn, Lauren, and Bunny.

And to those close: Harrison, Sarah, and Matt, and, of course, Harry.

Acknowledgments

My sincere thanks to Debby Kratovil, who started me on this crazy journey, and dear friends who are the wind beneath my wings: Julie Uhlhorn Riley, Nancy Arnold, Stacey Cimowsky, Amy Durham, Margueritte Jackson, Elizabeth Johnson, Candy Maley, Anna Orr, Maxine Watkins, and Laura Boyd—who also named this book!

Make Your Bed: Quilted Bed Runners, Pillows, and More to Suit Your Style
© 2011 by Leslee Evans

That Patchwork Place® is an imprint of Martingale & Company®.

Martingale & Company
19021 120th Ave. NE, Suite 102
Bothell, WA 98011-9511 USA
www.martingale-pub.com

Credits

President & CEO: Tom Wierzbicki
Editor in Chief: Mary V. Green
Managing Editor: Tina Cook
Developmental Editor: Karen Costello Soltys
Design Director: Stan Green
Technical Editor: Laurie Baker
Copy Editor: Marcy Heffernan
Production Manager: Regina Girard
Illustrator: Laurel Strand
Cover & Text Designer: Stan Green
Photographer: Brent Kane

Printed in China
16 15 14 13 12 11   8 7 6 5 4 3 2 1

Library of Congress Cataloging-in-Publication Data is available upon request.

ISBN: 978-1-60468-047-8

Mission Statement

Dedicated to providing quality products and service to inspire creativity.

Contents

WITHDRAWN

Introduction

Making my bed in the morning has never been my strong suit. But this book isn't about making your bed. It's about making your bed a piece of art. One that reflects your personality. One that can change with the seasons. One that sets your creativity free.

Start with a blank canvas, such as a white duvet or a textured matelasse bedspread. Then, splash on personality with a long strip of fabric—a bed runner that is pieced, quilted, and embellished with yummy, fun things like tassels and crystals that were formerly forbidden on bed quilts. Turn back the top sheet to reveal a band of color, toss on shams and a few pillows, and—bam! You have a beautiful bed!

While a bed runner is reminiscent of a traditional quilt, it's more like the blanket that is artfully tossed on the end of a bed in design magazines to give a space color and warmth. It's small enough to temper the "Oh my goodness, this is going to take forever!" fear. It gives you creative freedom because a bed runner is meant to be art, which grants it the privilege of providing the snuggly accent of a typical bed quilt or existing just for the sake of beauty. Plus, bed runners require a fraction of the materials used to make a standard quilt, so you can feel secure in the knowledge that if you don't love the finished product, it didn't cost you a fortune, either in fabric or time.

Each of the nine ensembles gives instructions for making a bed runner (with the exception of the "Sassy" ensemble runners, all of the runners fit a queen- or king-sized bed) and several accessories, like pillows, shams, and embellished sheets that match the runner. Four of the nine projects also give instructions for a "flip side," which is simply a complete second design on the back of the runner. Even some of the pillows can be flipped. The best part about a runner or pillow's flipability is how easily your bedroom can be transformed. A simple flip to the runner and pillows gives a whole new look!

Choices, choices, choices. With so much inspiration, I hope you find joy in making your bed every day!

~Leslee Evans

Basic Quiltmaking

Many quilters will skip this section and go right to the good stuff. I hope those of you who stopped by can learn something you didn't know before!

WHAT NOT TO DO!

Being a "recovering perfectionist," I must start with a few of my quilting pet peeves.

- Do not leave selvages on your fabric! Selvages stretch differently than the rest of the fabric, which can result in puckers and wonkiness in your quilt.
- Do not press seam allowances open unless specified in the pattern! Press both layers of fabric to one side. That way, if the piecing thread should break, a hole doesn't appear in the seam.
- Do not use the same old needle! Change your needle after every project.
- Do not expect yourself to be perfect! Quilting is an art that cherishes personal expression; the things you consider imperfections are really just character.

ABOUT FRONTS AND FLIP SIDES

The fronts and flip sides of the reversible runners in this book are designed to work together, but with a little mathematical ingenuity to resize the flip side, any flip side and front could go together. Keep these tips in mind:

- A flip-side design is different in nature than a front design. The front design often has borders or defined blocks, but the flip side must float on a field, because it's very difficult to get the flip side perfectly centered.
- The flip side needs to be 6" to 8" longer and wider on each side than the front for quilting. For this reason, the *unfinished* size of the runner flip side is given with the project instructions. The additional fabric will be trimmed away, so design accordingly.
- The binding fabric should coordinate with both sides of the project; however, if you get in a bind, a reversible binding can solve the problem (see page 84).

- The quilting needs to work for both sides, so consider the quilting design and thread color from both points of view. Match top and bobbin thread colors as closely as possible to avoid "pokies" (thread dots that poke through from the other side when the tension isn't quite right).

MAKING HALF-SQUARE-TRIANGLE UNITS

There are several good methods for making half-square triangles, but my favorite involves not cutting any triangles at all!

To make half-square-triangle units, mark a diagonal line from corner to corner on the wrong side of the lighter fabric square. Layer the marked square on the darker square, right sides together with the edges aligned. Stitch ¼" away from both sides of the drawn line. Cut the layered squares apart on the drawn line. Press the resulting two half-square-triangle units open, pressing the seam allowances toward the darker half or in the direction indicated. Measure the units to make sure they are the right size. They should be ½" larger than the desired finished size. If they are too big, trim two sides, making sure the diagonal meets at a point in the corner.

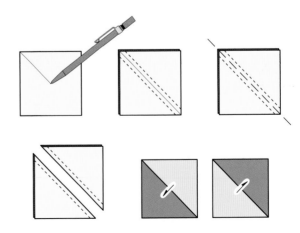

AVOIDING WAVY BORDERS

A surefire way to get wavy borders is to cut a generous length of border fabric and stitch it on without measuring. Fabric stretches, especially on the edges of a quilt. The instructions given here for borders with mitered corners and borders with butted corners will ensure your borders are straight and true.

Borders with Mitered Corners

1. Mark the seam allowances at the corners that will be mitered on the wrong side of the bed-runner top or pillow top and the border strips. Place a dot where the lines intersect.

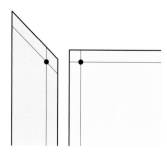

2. Lay the border piece over the top, right sides together. Insert the point of a pin through the dots to align them and align the edges of the top and border pieces; pin if desired. Starting at the point of the pin, sew a few stitches, and then backstitch, being careful not to sew into the seam allowance. Remove the pin. Continue stitching the rest of the seam. Press the seam allowances toward the border.

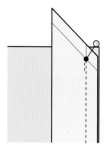

3. Repeat step 2 for the adjacent border piece, placing the first stitch right at the point where the seam line of the previous border piece starts. Repeat for any remaining border pieces.

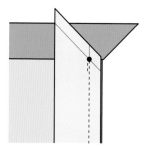

4. Fold the project in half diagonally, aligning the angled ends of the borders and the seam lines of the borders already stitched. Stitch the angled ends, starting right at the point where the border stitching meets. This seam is sewn on the bias, so take special care to not stretch the fabric.

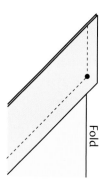

5. Unfold the top and press the seam allowances to one side.

Borders with Butted Corners

1. Measure the length of the runner *through the center*; cut two strips to this measurement. Pin-mark the center and quarter points of the runner edges and border strips.

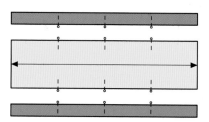

Measure through center of runner.
Mark half and quarter points.

2. Pin the borders to the sides of the runner, matching the pins and ends. Sew the borders in place, easing the edge as necessary. Press the seam allowances toward the border strips.

3. Measure the width of the runner through the center, including the side borders just added; cut two borders strips to this measurement. Attach the borders as described for the side borders. Press the seam allowances toward the border strips.

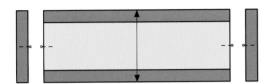

Measure center of runner including borders.
Mark half points.

MAKING THE QUILT SANDWICH

If the runner will be quilted by a professional machine quilter, do not make a quilt sandwich! The long-arm quilter needs the pieces to be separate.

1. Smooth the flip side or backing fabric right side down on a flat surface. Use a laser level or ruler to square up the edges. Tape down the edges with masking tape. The flip side should be smooth, but not pulled tight.

2. Layer the batting over the flip side and smooth out any wrinkles.

3. Layer the runner front over the batting, right side up and roughly centered. Use a ruler or a laser level to square up the blocks and sides.

4. Baste with thread every 4" to 6" using long running stitches, or use safety pins to pin through all three layers every 4" to 6". Start in the center and work toward the edges.

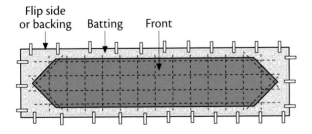

Flip side or backing   Batting   Front

BINDING

Although I prefer bias binding because of its stretchiness, most quilters prefer straight-grain double-fold binding because it takes less fabric and less time to cut. It's best to use bias binding when binding curves or when using striped fabric. The instructions for these projects use straight-grain binding unless otherwise noted. Because many of the bed runners have 135° corners, instructions and illustrations are also given for binding this angle as well as the more common 90° corner.

Attaching Binding

1. Sew the binding strips together at a 45° angle to make one long strip. Press the seam allowances open. Cut one end of the binding strip at a 45° angle. Press ¼" of the angled end toward the wrong side of the strip.

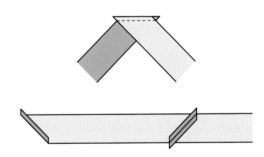

2. Fold the strip in half lengthwise, wrong sides together; press.

3. Beginning with the angled end and starting about halfway down the edge of the quilt, align the raw edges of the binding with the quilt edge. Leaving an 8" to 10" tail, sew the binding to the front of the quilt using the seam allowance designated in the pattern. At the corner, stop stitching one seam allowance width away from the edge. Cut the threads.

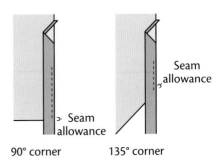

Seam allowance

Seam allowance

90° corner   135° corner

4. Turn the quilt and fold the binding straight up at a 90° angle so the fold forms a 45° angle (or half of the corner angle).

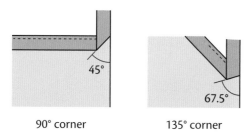

90° corner   135° corner

5. Fold the binding back down along the edge of the quilt, aligning the fold with the edge that was just stitched (or the corner of the quilt). Begin stitching at the edge of the quilt. Continue attaching the binding, sewing the remaining corners the same way.

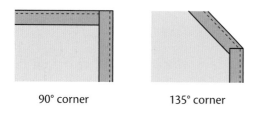

90° corner   135° corner

6. Finish stitching about 8" from the starting point and cut the threads. Tuck the end of the binding strip into the beginning and mark the 45° angle of the beginning strip on the ending strip. Trim the ending strip ¼" away from the marked seam to allow for the seam allowance.

7. Open up the beginning and ending strip so they lie flat and unfold the pressed edge at the beginning of the strip. With right sides together, match the marked line of the ending strip with the pressed line of the beginning strip and stitch the ends together on the line.

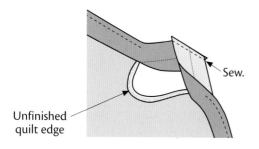

Unfinished quilt edge   Sew.

8. Refold the binding in half lengthwise and finish stitching it to the quilt.

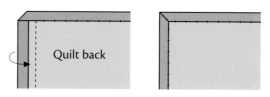

9. Fold the binding to the back of the quilt. With the folded edge covering the machine stitching, blindstitch the binding by hand, burying the stitches in the batting. At the corners, fold the back miter in the opposite direction from the front miter to make the miters less bulky.

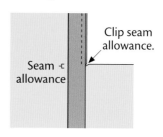

Quilt back

Binding Inside Corners

Inside corners are a bit different from outside corners. Here's how to get them perfect!

1. When you come to an inside corner, stop stitching the width of the seam allowance away from the corner and leave the needle down. Clip the seam allowance (of the quilt, not the binding) at a 45° angle, clipping from the corner just to the stitching.

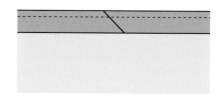

Seam allowance   Clip seam allowance.

2. Turn the quilt and pull the edge of the quilt straight, folding the quilt out of the way under the binding. Align the binding with the straightened edge and continue stitching the binding to the quilt.

MAKING PIPING

Piping is often used to finish the edges of pillows and shams. You can purchase ready-made piping or make your own following these instructions.

1. Sew the fabric strips together at a 45° angle and press the seam allowances open. Cut one end at a 45° angle and press the angled end ¼" to the wrong side of the strip.

2. Fold the fabric strip in half lengthwise, wrong sides together, aligning the raw edges and snugging the cord into the fold. Use a zipper foot to stitch as close to the cord as possible.

3. Starting about halfway down the edge of the pillow front, align the raw edges of the fabric-covered cord with the pillow edge. Leaving an 8" tail, sew the piping to the pillow, stitching as close to the cord as possible. At the corner, leave the needle down and clip the piping seam allowances up to the stitching.

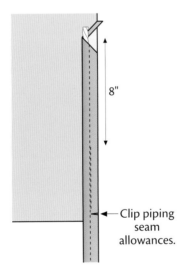

8"

Clip piping seam allowances.

4. Turn the pillow, align the piping with the next side, and continue stitching. Finish stitching about 8" from the starting point and cut the threads.

5. Overlap the end of the piping with the beginning tail about 3" and cut off the excess. Loosen the threads at each end of the piping. Tuck the end of the piping fabric strip into the beginning and mark the 45° angle on the ending strip. Trim the ending strip ¼" away from the marked seam for the seam allowance.

6. Open up the beginning and ending fabric strip so they lie flat and unfold the pressed edge at the beginning of the strip. With right sides together and the cord out of the way, match the marked line of the ending strip with the pressed line of the beginning strip and stitch the ends together on the line.

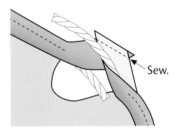

Sew.

7. Trim the ends of the piping so they butt, refold the piping fabric, and stitch the remainder of the seam.

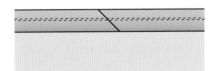

8. To sew the piped side to the other side of the pillow or sham, sew with the piped side on top, right sides together, using your fingernail to press the cord tightly into the piping fabric so the zipper foot can stitch as close to the cord as possible.

Basic Bed Making

Beautiful and comfortable beds are the result of layers.

Artistically, the layers start at the floor with a dust ruffle, which can be solid or patterned, ruffled, pleated or tailored, or even layered itself with lace or a gauzy fabric. Next, the practical takes over with a cushy mattress pad topped with quality sheets. The top sheet can be embellished in many creative ways, and in the old German tradition, is put on the bed with the right side down so that the right side of the border shows when it's folded back. The next layer is your blank canvas, the comforter or duvet. Choose a solid neutral color, either smooth or with a texture like matelasse, to best showcase your runner and pillows and allow design flexibility. Turn the comforter and top sheet down about two feet, leaving plenty of room for pillows at the head of the bed. Then, layer pillows at will! Cased pillows, shams, accent pillows of all shapes and sizes—have fun with it! Finally, drape a runner at the foot of the bed. Your bed is beautiful!

EMBELLISHING SHEETS AND PILLOWCASES

Embellishing your sheets and pillowcases with soft lace, fancy decorative stitching, or a colorful fabric band is a great way to easily jazz up your bed.

Adding Decorative Stitching

Some sewing machines have wonderful decorative stitches available at the touch of a button. Simply choose your stitch and sew away!

You don't need a fancy embroidery machine to perk up your bedding. You can trim premade pillowcases and sheets with straight, zigzag, and free-motion stitching.

Trimming with Lace or Ribbon

Stitching lace to the outer edge. Starting at a side seam line, butt the lace directly to the edge of the sheet or pillowcase. Using a zigzag stitch and matching thread, catch the edges of the bedding and lace to join them. Hand finish the ends of the lace if needed.

Stitching lace or ribbon within the hem. Usually, there is a natural place to stitch lace or ribbon in the hem. Some have a hemline seam that you can easily follow and some have piping embellishments already added. Just follow your creative instincts! Turn under the end of the trim and start stitching at a seam line using a straight or zigzag stitch, depending on the type of lace or ribbon. Turn under the end of the trim as you finish and sew the ends together by hand or machine.

Keep embellishments soft. They may touch your face while you're sleeping.

Common Flat-Sheet and Pillowcase Sizes

Note that sheet sizes vary slightly with brand and quality, so always measure before starting a project.

	Flat Sheet	Pillowcase
Twin	66" x 96"	20" x 30"
Full	81" x 96"	20" x 30"
Queen	90" x 102"	20" x 34"
King/ California King	108" x 102"	20" x 40"

Adding a Fabric Band to a Flat Sheet

There are an abundance of fabric-band options! This one is a simple 6"-wide fabric band finished with a French seam resembling flat piping. To punch up this simple band, add lace, ribbon, or a second fabric strip in the French seam.

Materials

Purchased flat sheet

Fabric for band. The band fabric can be cut across the width of the fabric and seamed together to achieve the required length, or you can cut it on the *lengthwise grain* if you prefer to avoid a seam.

> Twin: ¾ yard (seamed) or 2⅛ yards (seamless)
>
> Full: 1¼ yards (seamed) or 2½ yards (seamless)
>
> Queen: 1¼ yards (seamed) or 2¾ yards (seamless)
>
> King: 1¼ yards (seamed) or 3¼ yards (seamless)

Preparing the Sheet

1. Wash and press the sheet.
2. Square up the bottom edge by folding the sheet in half lengthwise twice. Align the folded edges on your cutting mat and trim off the hem straight. Trim as close to the hem as possible. This is now the top of the sheet.
3. Remove the side hems from the trimmed end to 6" above the trimmed end.

Making and Attaching the Fabric Band

1. Measure the width of the top edge of the sheet, including the folded out hem on each side. If there are no side hems, add 4" to the "sheet width" measurement.
2. Cut the fabric for the band into strips, 12½" x the sheet width. If you cut the strips across the width of the fabric, join the ends of the strips if needed to achieve the sheet width. Fold the strip in half lengthwise, wrong sides together.
3. Align the fabric-band raw edges with the top edge of the sheet, right sides together, and stitch using a ¼" seam allowance. If the sheet is unhemmed on the sides, leave a 2" tail of the band fabric at each end for hemming. Press the seam allowances toward the sheet.

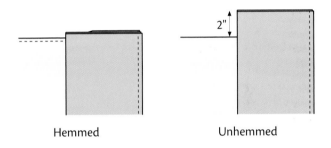

Hemmed   Unhemmed

4. Place the sheet right side down on your work surface. Flip the band over onto the sheet, snugging the seam allowance raw edges into the new fold. Stitch in the ditch of the band seam line to enclose the seam allowances.

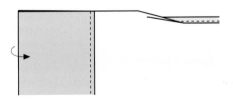

Flip band back along seam allowance.

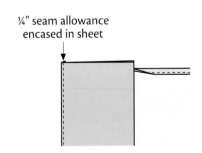

¼" seam allowance encased in sheet

5. Flip the band back to the right side and press the enclosed seam allowance (which is now on the right side of the sheet below the band) toward the sheet. Finish the sides to match the original side hems of the sheet, or if the sheet is unhemmed, hem the band by folding the tail flush with the edge with the sheet, tucking under the raw end to the fold, and stitching in place.

Making a Pillowcase with a Fabric Band

You can make pillowcases with a fabric body and band, or you can start with a purchased pillowcase.

Materials (for one pillowcase)

Purchased pillowcase *or* 1 yard of fabric for body for standard- or queen-size or 1⅛ yards of fabric for king size

½ yard of fabric for band

Cutting

From the body fabric, cut:

Standard: 1 rectangle, 25" x 41"

Queen: 1 rectangle, 29" x 41"

King: 1 rectangle, 35" x 41"

From the band fabric, cut:

1 rectangle, 12½" x 41", *or* for a purchased pillowcase, 1 rectangle, 12½" x pillowcase width (see step 2)

Making the Pillowcase Body

1. Wash and press the purchased pillowcase and/or body and band fabrics.
2. *If you're using a purchased pillowcase,* cut off the hemmed edge at the open end of the pillowcase. Measure the pillowcase width at the open end. Multiply this measurement by 2 and add 1" for seam allowances to get the "pillowcase width" needed for cutting the band.

   If you're making the pillowcase body, choose one of these options:

   Option 1: Regular seams. Fold the body fabric in half, right sides together, to make a rectangle measuring 20½" wide and 25" (standard), 29" (queen), or 35" (king) long. Stitch the side seam using a ½" seam allowance. Serge or zigzag finish the seam. Stitch and finish one end in the same manner.

Option 2: French seams. Fold the fabric in half, wrong sides together, to make a rectangle measuring 20½" wide and 25" (standard), 29" (queen), or 35" (king) long. Stitch the side seam using a ¼" seam allowance. Trim 1/16" to ⅛" from the seam allowance and press it to one side. Turn the pillowcase wrong side out and stitch ¼" from the previous seam line to encase the raw edges. Turn the pillowcase to the right side and press. Stitch one end in the same manner.

Adding the Band

1. Sew the ends of the band fabric, right sides together, using a ½" seam allowance. Fold the piece in half lengthwise and press.
2. Align the band and pillowcase raw edges, right sides together and matching the side seams. Stitch using a ¼" seam allowance. Press the seam allowances toward the pillowcase body.
3. Flip the band inside the pillowcase, snugging the seam allowance raw edges into the new fold. Stitch in the ditch of the band seam line to enclose the seam allowances.

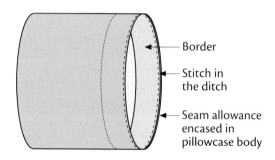

Border

Stitch in the ditch

Seam allowance encased in pillowcase body

4. Flip the band back to the right side and press the enclosed seam allowance (which is now on the right side of the pillowcase below the band) toward the pillowcase body.

PILLOWS AND SHAMS

Shams are the artist's backdrop, and pillows add texture, color, and dimension to the head of your bed. With all the beautiful fabrics available, it's easy to create stunning pillows and shams. Add fringe, cording, or tassels to punch them up even more!

The Easiest Pillow Ever

This pillow's front can be pieced and lined or pieced and quilted, or it can be just a single piece of fabric. The back opening is overlapped 3". The instructions are for making a 16" x 16" pillow, but they can be easily altered to any size you may want to make. If you'd like a button closure on the flip side, refer to "The Still Easy but Reversible Pillow" (at right).

Materials

⅝ yard of fabric for pillow front and back *or* 1 fat quarter of fabric for front and ½ yard of different fabric for back

16" x 16" square pillow form

18" x 18" piece of plain cotton or muslin for front lining (for pieced or quilted front only)

18" x 18" piece of batting (for quilted front only)

2 yards of fringe or lace or 2 yards of cording and ¼ yard of fabric to cover cording (optional)

4 tassels for corners (optional)

Cutting

From the front fabric, cut:
1 square, 17" x 17"

From the back fabric, cut:
2 rectangles, 17" x 12"

Making the Pillow

1. If the front is pieced, either line or quilt it to protect the seams on the inside of the pillow. To line it, center the pieced front over the lining square, baste around the edges, and then trim the lining even with the pillow top. To quilt it, center the pieced front over the batting and lining, baste around the edges, and then quilt. Trim the batting and lining to 17" x 17" (refer to "The Fudge Factor" on page 15).

2. If desired, sew fringe or cording to the edges of the front piece using a scant ½" seam allowance or baste tassels ½" in from each corner.

3. Turn under one 17"-long edge of each back piece 1" twice and stitch close to the first folded edge.

4. With right sides together, place the back pieces on the front piece so the hemmed edges overlap 3" at the center and the outer raw edges are aligned; pin. Stitch around the pillow edges using a ½" seam allowance.

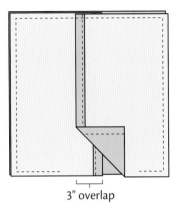

3" overlap

5. Trim the corners at an angle. Turn the pillow cover right side out and press. Insert the pillow form through the opening in the back.

The Still Easy but Reversible Pillow

This 17" x 17" pillow features a bound edge and a flip side (never to be called "the back"!) that has a button closure. Each side can be made with a different fabric to give you options when you make your bed. If you'd like to add fringe, cording, or tassels, follow the instructions in "The Easiest Pillow Ever" (at left) for the front and the instructions that follow for the flip side.

Materials

⅝ yard of fabric for front and flip side *or* 1 fat quarter of fabric for front and ½ yard of a different fabric for flip side

18" x 18" piece of plain cotton or muslin for lining (for pieced and/or quilted front only)

14½" x 18" piece of plain cotton or muslin for lining (for pieced and/or quilted flip side only)

7" x 18" piece of plain cotton or muslin for lining (for pieced and/or quilted flip side only)

¼ yard of fabric for binding

18" x 18" piece of batting (for quilted front only)

14½" x 18" piece of batting (for quilted flip side only)

7" x 18" piece of batting (for quilted flip side only)

⅛ yard of lightweight fusible interfacing

3 same-sized buttons, ⅝" to 1¼" in diameter

16" x 16" square pillow form

Cutting

From the front fabric, cut:
> 1 square, 17" x 17"

From the flip-side fabric, cut:
> 1 rectangle, 15½" x 17"
> 1 rectangle, 9½" x 17"

From the binding fabric, cut:
> 2 strips, 3⅛" x 42"

From the interfacing, cut:
> 2 strips, 1½" x 17"

Making the Pillow Front

If the front is pieced, either line or quilt it to protect the seams on the inside of the pillow. To line it, center the pieced front over the lining square, baste around the edges, and then trim the lining even with the pillow top. To quilt it, center the pieced front over the batting and lining, baste around the edges, and then quilt. Trim the batting and lining to 17" x 17" (refer to "The Fudge Factor" on page 15).

Making the Flip Side

1. To make the button band, fuse a strip of interfacing to the wrong side of one 17"-long edge of each flip-side piece. Fold the interfaced edge over 1½" and press. Fold over 1½" again and press.

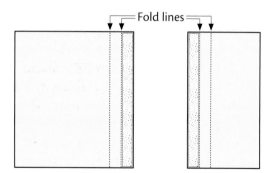

Fold lines

2. *If you're not quilting or lining the flip side,* stitch close to the first folded edge on each button band.

   If you are quilting or lining the flip side, unfold the interfaced button band once and line up a piece of batting and/or lining to the edge of the fold (the 14½" x 18" lining and batting pieces will go on the 15½" x 17" fabric pieces). Refold the button band 1½" over the batting and/or lining and stitch close to the edge to hem. Stay stitch

around the raw edges of each piece, and then trim the batting and lining even with the top. Quilt both flip-side pieces, if desired.

3. On the wider of the two flip-side pieces, mark three vertical buttonholes on the button band, ¾" from the long edge, placing one in the center and one 4" from each side of the center. Make the buttonholes.

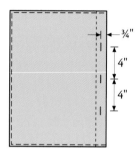

Assembling the Pillow

1. With wrong sides together and the hemmed edge toward the center, place the narrower flip-side piece on one end of the front piece with the raw edges aligned. Center the wider flip-side piece on the opposite end, overlapping the narrower piece by 1½" so the bands align; pin. If needed, trim any extra fabric of the wider piece flush with the front. Stitch around the pillow edges using a scant ½" seam allowance.

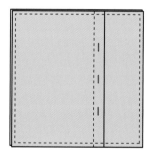

2. Bind the pillow edges using 3⅛" binding strips and a ½" seam allowance for a ½" finished binding. Refer to "Binding" (on page 7) as needed.

3. Mark the button locations on the narrower flip-side piece to correspond to the buttonholes and sew the buttons to the band. Insert the pillow form into the cover.

The Fudge Factor

Because quilting tends to shrink the size of the quilted pieces, your pillow front may not measure exactly 17" x 17" after quilting. Just trim the oversized backing and batting to 17" x 17", leaving the edges of the quilted top a little shy. Because you're using a ½" seam allowance (to turn or bind the edges), you'll have a little bit of fudge room on each edge. (I do SO love fudge!)

Shams: The Same, but Different!

Shams are made exactly like pillows but with different dimensions and an additional top-stitching line to make the flange. The instructions make a standard-sized sham, but if you prefer a different-sized sham, adding a few inches in the right places is all it takes.

Common Sham Sizes		
	Pillow Form	Sham Cover
Standard	20" x 26"	26" x 32"
Queen	20" x 30"	26" x 36"
King	20" x 36"	26" x 42"
European	27" x 27"	33" x 33"

Materials (for one standard-sized sham)

For The Easiest Sham Ever:

⅞ yard of fabric *each* for sham front and flip side

3½ yards of cording and ½ yard of fabric to cover cording (optional)

3½ yards of fringe or lace (optional)

Standard-sized pillow

For The Still Easy but Reversible Sham:

⅞ yard of fabric *each* for sham front and flip side

28" x 34" piece of fabric for lining (for pieced and/or quilted front only)

25½" x 28" piece of fabric for lining (for pieced and/or quilted flip side only)

13" x 28" piece of fabric for lining (for quilted flip side only)

½ yard of fabric for binding

28" x 34" piece of batting (for quilted front only)

25½" x 28" piece of batting (for quilted flip side only)

13" x 28" piece of batting (for quilted flip side only)

⅞ yard of lightweight fusible interfacing

3 same-sized buttons, ⅝" to 1¼" in diameter

Standard-sized pillow

Cutting

For both types of shams

From the front fabric, cut:
1 rectangle, 27" x 33"

For The Easiest Sham Ever:

From the flip-side fabric, cut:
1 rectangle, 27" x 25½"
1 rectangle, 27" x 14½"

For The Still Easy but Reversible Sham:

From the flip-side fabric, cut:
1 rectangle, 27" x 26½"
1 rectangle, 27" x 14"

From the interfacing, cut:
2 strips, 1½" x 27"

From the binding fabric, cut:
3 strips, 3⅛" x 42"

Making the Sham

1. For The Easiest Sham Ever, follow the instructions for "The Easiest Pillow Ever" (page 13). For The Still Easy but Reversible Sham, follow the instructions for "The Still Easy but Reversible Pillow" (page 13), but make the buttonholes 6" apart.

2. After turning the sham, make the flange by topstitching 3" from the edges of the sham.

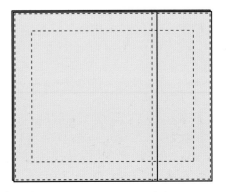

MakeYourBed
CHARMING

This rich rose fabric was made to grace a garden cottage! The classic Irish Chain on one side of the bed runner and simple floating leaves on the flip side are soft and romantic, touched with quaint lace trim and scalloped edges. If you don't want to tackle the scalloped edge, leave it straight. It will look fabulous either way.

Rose Irish Chain Runner

Finished Runner: 31½" x 115½" • Finished Block: 6" x 6"

MATERIALS

Yardage is based on 42"-wide fabric. Materials for the flip side are given on page 21.

3⅜ yards of red tone-on-tone print for blocks, inner and outer borders, and binding

1¾ yards of white-and-red floral for blocks and inner border

3½ yards of fabric for backing (only needed if not using the pieced flip side)

36" x 120" piece of batting

8 yards of ⅜"-wide picot-edge ecru lace for border trim

4½" x 12" piece of paper for scallop template

Marking pen

CUTTING

From the red tone-on-tone print, cut:

16 strips, 2½" x 42"; crosscut *4 of the strips* into:
22 rectangles, 2½" x 6½"
4 squares, 2½" x 2½"
8 strips, 5" x 42"

Enough 2½"-wide bias strips to yield a 320" strip after piecing

From the red-and-white floral, cut:

5 strips, 6½" x 42"; crosscut into 25 squares, 6½" x 6½"

9 strips, 2½" x 42"

MAKING THE NINE PATCH BLOCKS

1. Sew the red tone-on-tone and red-and-white floral 2½" x 42" strips together along the long edges to make strip sets A and B as shown. Press the seam allowances toward the red strips. Crosscut the strip sets into the number of 2½"-wide segments indicated.

Strip set A.
Make 5. Cut 70 segments.

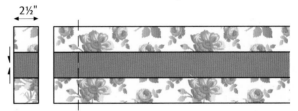

Strip set B.
Make 2. Cut 26 segments.

2. Sew A segments to opposite sides of a B segment to make a Nine Patch block. Press the seam allowances toward the A segments. Repeat to make a total of 26 blocks. Set aside the remainder of the A segments for the inner border.

 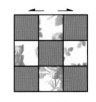

Nine Patch block.
Make 26.

ASSEMBLING THE RUNNER TOP

1. Sew Nine Patch blocks to opposite sides of a red-and-white floral square. Press the seam allowances toward the Nine Patch blocks. Sew a red 2½" x 6½" rectangle to each end of the row. Press the seam allowances toward the rectangles. Repeat to make a total of nine of row A.

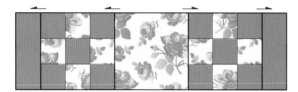

Row A.
Make 9.

2. Sew red-and-white floral squares to opposite sides of a Nine Patch block. Press the seam allowances toward the Nine Patch block. Sew an A segment you set aside earlier to each end of the row. Press the seam allowances toward the red-and-white squares. Repeat to make a total of eight of row B.

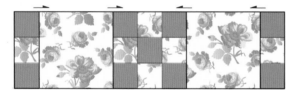

Row B.
Make 8.

3. Join two red 2½" squares, two red 2½" x 6½" rectangles, and one remaining A segment as shown. Press the seam allowances in the directions indicated. Repeat to make a total of two of row C.

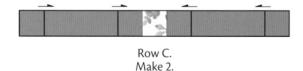

Row C.
Make 2.

4. Refer to the runner assembly diagram to alternately join the A and B rows. Add the C rows to the ends of the runner. Refer to "Borders with Butted Corners" (page 6) to sew the red 5"-wide outer-border strips to the quilt top.

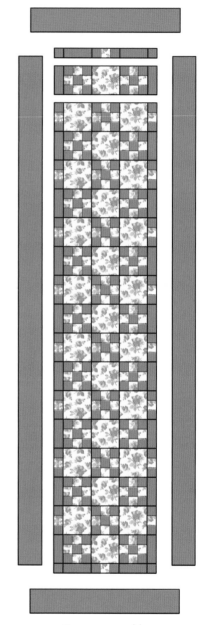

Runner assembly

5. To add the lace, mark a guideline on the outer border ¾" from the border seam line, or use a length of ¾"-wide painter's tape as a guide. Stitch the top edge of the lace along the guideline using a zigzag stitch, turning under the end

18

and overlapping the beginning of the lace to finish. The bottom edge of the trim will remain unstitched.

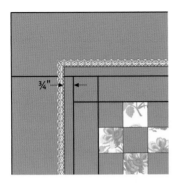

FINISHING

If you're making the bed runner reversible, refer to "Runner Flip Side: Scattered Leaves" (page 20) to make the flip side of the runner before proceeding. If you're not making the bed runner reversible, use the backing fabric in place of the flip side in the following instructions.

1. Refer to "Making the Quilt Sandwich" (page 7) to layer the bed-runner top, batting, and flip side (or backing fabric); baste the layers together.

2. Quilt the layers together, starting at the center of the bed runner and working toward the edges. In the runner shown, I stabilized the quilt by quilting the diagonal lines with red thread. Then, I stitched in the ditch around the border and at the edge of the lace. Using ivory thread, I quilted the curves in the Nine Patch block squares and added a fleur-de-lis design in the red-and-white floral squares. After quilting, trim the batting and flip side even with the runner top.

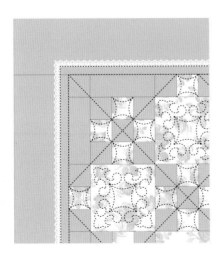

3. To make the scalloped border, fold the 4½" x 12" piece of paper in half to make a piece that is 4½" x 6". Trace the runner scallop pattern (page 27) onto the paper; cut away and discard the piece indicated. Unfold the template.

4. Place the template on one long edge of the outer border so the template ends are aligned with the center of the red-and-white floral squares and the straight edge is aligned with the border seam as shown. Trace the curved edge onto the outer border. Reposition the template to mark the next scallop. Continue in this manner to mark both long side borders. Mark two curves on each short end border, positioning the template so it aligns with the center of the floral square as before. Mark the corner curves using a 7"-diameter circle. A plate or circle template works well for this.

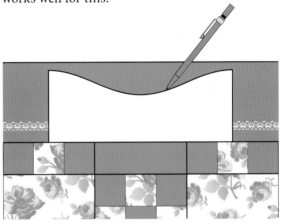

5. Stitch just inside the drawn line, and then trim on the drawn line.

6. Bind the edges using the 2½"-wide bias strips and a ⅜" seam allowance. Refer to "Binding" (page 7) as needed.

Runner Flip Side: Scattered Leaves

Unfinished Runner: 34½" x 121½" • Finished Block: 7½" x 7½"

MATERIALS

Yardage is based on 42"-wide fabric. Binding, backing, and batting yardages are given with the "Rose Irish Chain Runner" materials list on page 17.

4 yards of red tone-on-tone print

⅝ yard of red-and-white floral

CUTTING

From the red tone-on-tone print, cut:

2 strips, 3⅜" x 42"; crosscut into 20 squares,
3⅜" x 3⅜"

2 strips, 3" x 42"; crosscut into 20 squares, 3" x 3"

2 rectangles, 8" x 9¼"

3 rectangles, 8" x 10¼"

2 rectangles, 8" x 11¼"

2 rectangles, 8" x 12¼"

1 rectangle, 8" x 13¼"

1 rectangle, 8" x 14¼"

2 rectangles, 8" x 15¼"

2 rectangles, 8" x 16¼"

3 rectangles, 8" x 17¼"

2 rectangles, 8" x 18¼"

2 strips, 15½" x 34½"

1 strip, 3½" x 34½"

2 strips, 4½" x 34½"

1 strip, 5½" x 34½"

From the red-and-white floral, cut:

2 strips, 3⅜" x 42"; crosscut into 20 squares,
3⅜" x 3⅜"

3 strips, 3" x 42"; crosscut into 30 squares, 3" x 3"

2 strips, 1" x 42"; crosscut into 10 rectangles,
1" x 5"

MAKING THE LEAF BLOCKS

1. Draw a diagonal line from corner to corner on the wrong side of each red-and-white floral 3⅜" square. Layer each marked square over a red tone-on-tone square, right sides together. Refer to "Making Half-Square-Triangle Units" (page 5) to make 40 half-square-triangle units. Press the seam allowances toward the red print.

2. To make the stem squares, draw a diagonal line from corner to corner on the right side of 10 red tone-on-tone 3" squares. With right sides

together, align the long raw edge of a red-and-white floral 1" x 5" rectangle with the drawn line of a marked square; stitch ¼" away from the marked line. Cut on the drawn line. Press the seam allowances toward the rectangle. Place the cut-off triangle along the rectangle long raw edge, right sides together, making sure to leave the same amount of the first triangle exposed on each short edge of the cut-off triangle; sew ¼" from the long edges. Press the seam allowances toward the stem and trim the stem ends even with the square. The square should measure 3" x 3". Repeat to make a total of 10 stem squares.

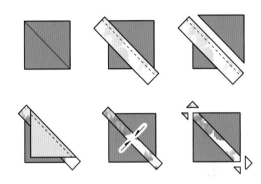

3. Arrange one stem square, three red-and-white floral 3" squares, one red 3" square, and four half-square-triangle units into three horizontal rows as shown. Sew the squares in each row together. Press the seam allowances as indicated. Sew the rows together. Press the seam allowances toward the middle row. Repeat to make a total of 10 blocks.

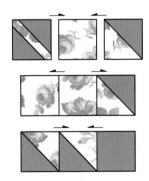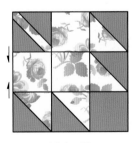

Make 10.

ASSEMBLING AND FINISHING

1. Refer to the runner assembly diagram to lay out the leaf blocks and the red tone-on-tone rectangles and strips as shown. Sew the leaf blocks to the 8"-long rectangles to make strips, and then sew the leaf-block strips and red tone-on-tone 34½"-wide strips together. If you want to play with the order, please do so. There is no "right" layout!

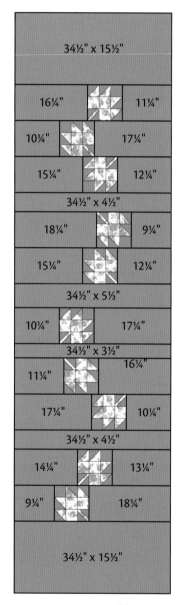

Runner assembly

2. Refer to the finishing instructions for "Rose Irish Chain Runner" (page 19) to layer, quilt, and bind the runner.

Rose Irish Chain Pillow

Finished Pillow: 21" x 21"

MATERIALS

Yardage is based on 42"-wide fabric unless otherwise noted.

1 yard of red-and-white floral for blocks and flip side

⅔ yard of red tone-on-tone print for blocks, border, and binding

2½ yards of ⅜"-wide picot-edge ecru lace

24" x 24" piece of plain cotton or muslin for front lining

24" x 24" piece of batting

⅔ yard of 20"-wide lightweight fusible interfacing

3 same-sized buttons, ⅝" to 1¼" in diameter

20" x 20" square pillow form

CUTTING

From the red tone-on-tone print, cut:

> 1 strip, 2½" x 42"
>
> 2 strips, 3¾" x 42"; crosscut each strip into:
>
> > 1 strip, 3¾" x 21" (2 total)
> >
> > 1 strip, 3¾" x 14½" (2 total)
>
> 3 strips, 3⅛" x 42"

From the red-and-white floral, cut:

> 1 strip, 2½" x 42"
>
> 1 rectangle, 17" x 21"
>
> 1 rectangle, 12" x 21"
>
> 1 square, 6½" x 6½"
>
> 4 squares, 4½" x 4½"

From the interfacing, cut:

> 2 strips, 1½" x 21"

MAKING THE PILLOW

1. Sew the red tone-on-tone and red-and-white floral 2½" x 42" strips together along the long edges to make a strip set. Press the seam allowances toward the red strip. Crosscut the strip set into 12 segments, 2½" wide.

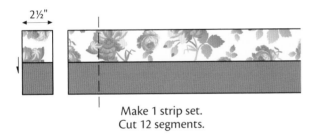

2½"

Make 1 strip set.
Cut 12 segments.

2. Sew three segments together as shown. Press the seam allowances toward the center segment. Repeat to make a total of four units.

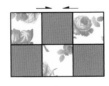

Make 4.

3. Refer to the pillow assembly diagram at right to arrange the units from step 2 and the red-and-white floral 4½" and 6½" squares into three horizontal rows as shown. Sew the pieces in each row together. Press the seam allowances toward the units from step 2. Sew the rows together. Press the seam allowances toward the center row.

4. Sew the red tone-on-tone 3¾" x 14½" border strips to the sides of the pillow center. Press the seam allowances toward the strips. Join the red tone-on-tone 3¾" x 21" border strips to the top and bottom of the pillow center. Press the seam allowances toward the strips.

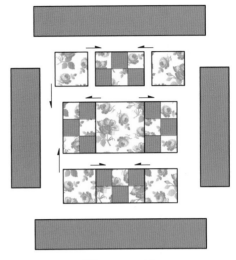

Pillow assembly

5. Mark a guideline on the border ¾" from the border seam line or use a length of ¾"-wide painter's tape as a guide. Stitch the top edge of the lace along the guideline using a zigzag stitch, turning under the end and overlapping the beginning of the lace to finish. The bottom edge of the trim will remain unstitched.

6. Refer to "Making the Quilt Sandwich" (page 7) to layer the front lining piece, batting, and pieced top; baste the layers together. Quilt, referring to the bed-runner quilting diagram (page 19), if desired.

7. Using the remaining red-and-white floral rectangles, refer to "Making the Flip Side" of "The Still Easy but Reversible Pillow" (page 13) to make the unquilted pillow back.

8. Stitch the pillow top to the pillow back, wrong sides together, using a scant ½" seam allowance. Bind the edges with the red tone-on-tone 3⅛"-wide strips using a ½" seam allowance.

9. Insert the pillow form into the cover.

Scallops-and-Lace Pillowcase

Finished Pillowcase: 20" x 28¼"

MATERIALS (for one pillowcase)

Yardage is based on 42"-wide fabric.

¾ yard of red-and-white floral for pillowcase body

⅝ yard of red tone-on-tone print for scalloped band

1¼ yards of ⅜"-wide picot-edge ecru lace

9" x 20" piece of paper

CUTTING

From the red-and-white floral, cut:
    1 rectangle, 21¼" x 41"

From the red tone-on-tone print, cut:
    2 strips, 9½" x 41"

MAKING THE SCALLOPED BAND

1. Fold the paper in half as shown above right to make a piece 9" x 10". Fold this piece into thirds to make a piece about 3⅓" x 9", folding the right edge in first, and then the left edge. The first fold should now be on the right-hand side.

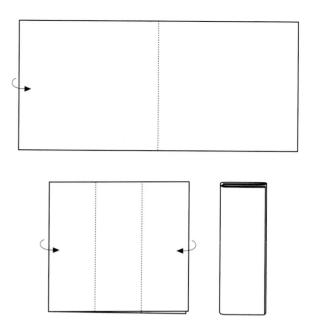

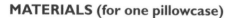

2. With the paper still folded, trace the pillowcase scallop pattern (page 26) onto the paper, making sure that the high point of the scallop is at the first folded edge; cut away and discard the piece indicated. Unfold the template.

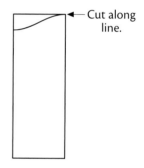

Cut along line.

3. Fold one of the red tone-on-tone strips in half crosswise, right sides together, to make a piece 9½" x 20½"; crease the fold. Place the scallop template on the strip with one straight end at the crease and the bottom edges aligned; mark the scallops. Flip the strip over and mark the scallops on the other side in the same manner.

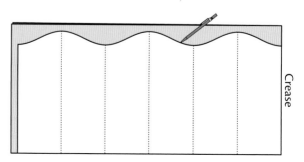

Crease

24

4. To attach the lace, mark a guideline on the strip 3" from the unmarked edge. Position the top edge of the lace on the guideline with the picot edge pointed toward the scalloped edge. Stitch the top edge of the lace in place using a zigzag stitch. The picot edge will remain unstitched.

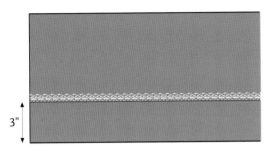

5. With right sides together and using a ½" seam allowance, sew the ends of the marked strip together to make a tube. Press the seam allowances open. Repeat with the unmarked red tone-on-tone strip.

6. Place the tubes right sides together, aligning the side seams. Stitch along the marked scalloped line. Trim ¼" from the stitching, clip the curves, turn the band right side out, and press.

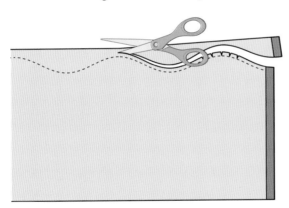

7. Refer to "Making a Pillowcase with a Fabric Band" (page 12) to make the body of the pillowcase from the red-and-white floral rectangle. Attach the band to the open end.

Scallops-and-Lace Sheet

MATERIALS (for a queen-size sheet)

Yardage is based on 42"-wide fabric.

Purchased queen-size flat sheet

1 yard of red-and-white floral for seamed outer band *or* 3 yards for seamless band

¾ yard of red tone-on-tone print for seamed scalloped band *or* 3 yards for seamless band

3 yards of ⅜"-wide picot-edge ecru lace

4" x 20" piece of paper

CUTTING

Measure the width of the top edge of the sheet and add 6". This is the "sheet width" measurement. For a queen-size sheet, this should be about 96".

From the red-and-white floral, cut:
  1 strip, 10½" x sheet width, for seamless band *or*
  3 strips, 10½" x 42", for seamed band

From the red tone-on-tone print, cut:
  2 strips, 4½" x sheet width, for seamless band *or*
  5 strips, 4½" x 42", for seamed band

MAKING THE BANDS

1. For the red-and-white floral accent band, if necessary, join the ends of the strips to make a strip measuring 1½" x sheet width. Fold the strip in half lengthwise, wrong sides together, and press.

2. For the red tone-on-tone scalloped band, if necessary, join the ends of the red strips to make two strips measuring 4½" x sheet width.

3. Refer to step 1 of "Scallops-and-Lace Pillowcase" (page 24) to make the paper template, or use the same template and trim it where indicated for the sheet. Unfold the template.

4. Place the template on the wrong side of one of the red tone-on-tone strips, aligning the template with the bottom edge and one end of the strip; mark the scallops. Move the template along the strip and continue marking scallops until the entire length has been marked.

5. To attach the lace, mark a guideline on the right side of the same red strip, 1" from the unmarked edge. Position the top edge of the lace on the guideline with the picot edge pointed toward the scalloped edge. Stitch the top edge of the lace in place using a zigzag stitch, turning under the end and overlapping the beginning of the lace to finish. The picot edge will remain unstitched.

6. Place the red tone-one-tone strips right sides together and stitch along the marked scallop line. Trim ¼" from the stitching, clip the curves, turn the band right side out, and press.

FINISHING

1. Prepare the sheet as instructed in "Preparing the Sheet" (page 11).

2. Lay the red-and-white floral accent band on a flat surface. Place the scalloped band over it with the lace facing up, aligning the raw edges. Layer the top edge of the sheet over the bands, wrong side up with the raw edges aligned. Stitch through all of the layers using a ¼" seam allowance.

3. Refer to steps 4 and 5 of "Making and Attaching the Fabric Band" (page 11) to finish the sheet.

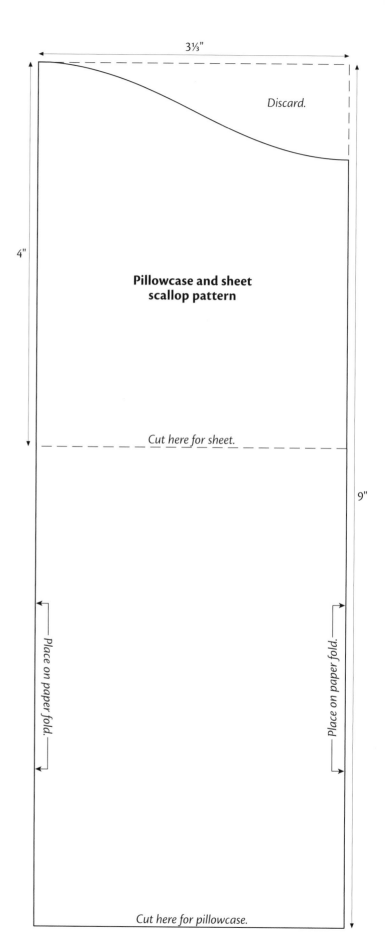

Pillowcase and sheet scallop pattern

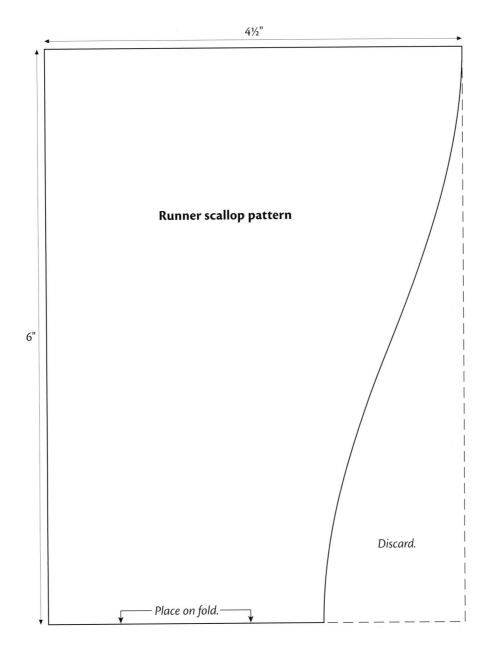

4½"

6"

Runner scallop pattern

Discard.

Place on fold.

Make Your Bed CLASSIC

Pattern and texture make this quilt a standout! The flip side showcases suiting fabrics, pinpoint oxford shirting, and red power ties—a perfect complement for the houndstooth patchwork pattern. Tailored boxed shams with contrasting cording complete the classic look. Be aware that the pieces will need to be dry cleaned and not washed because of the wool and silk fibers used in these fabrics.

Houndstooth Runner

Finished Runner: 26" x 98" • Finished Block: 3" x 3"

MATERIALS

Yardage is based on 42"-wide fabric unless otherwise noted. Materials for the flip side are given on page 32.

3 yards of red solid for blocks and border

2½ yards of white solid for blocks

½ yard of 58"-wide dark gray wool or wool-blend suiting fabric for binding

3⅛ yards of fabric for backing (only needed if not using the pieced flip side)

30" x 103" piece of batting

Lightweight printer paper or tracing paper

CUTTING

From the *lengthwise grain* of the red solid, cut:
  2 strips, 2¾" x 93½"

From the remainder of the red solid, cut:
  64 squares, 3½" x 3½"
  156 rectangles, 1¾" x 6"
  120 rectangles, 1¾" x 3"
  2 strips, 2¾" x 26"

From the white solid, cut:
  45 squares, 3½" x 3½"
  168 rectangles, 1¾" x 6"
  96 rectangles, 1¾" x 3"

From the dark gray suiting fabric, cut:
  5 strips, 2½" x 58"

MAKING THE STRIPED BLOCKS

All the blocks in this quilt are made using the same foundation pattern, but they're pieced in two different arrangements: one with a red stripe in the center and one with a white stripe in the center. Before starting, set the stitch length on your sewing machine to 12 stitches per inch or shorter to make removing the paper foundation easier.

1. Copy the foundation patterns (page 39) onto lightweight printer or tracing paper. Make 108 copies total: 60 copies for the red striped blocks and 48 copies for the white striped blocks.

2. To make the red striped blocks, center a white 6"-long rectangle over a red 3"-long rectangle, right sides together.

3. With the printed side up, place a pattern over the layered rectangles so that area 2 on the pattern is centered on the white fabric rectangle. Stitch on the line between areas 1 and 2.

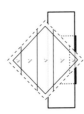

4. Flip the pattern over, open the red rectangle to the right side, and press along the seam line with your fingernail. Make sure the seam is pressed flat.

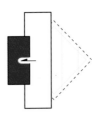

Design Details

When I began this quilt, I thought it would be easy to make. After all, it's all straight-line sewing, right? The problem is, if the lines are just a little bit off, the eye picks up the mistakes, and the quilt looks really wonky. Happily, it's easy to maintain accuracy with paper-foundation piecing. Just pay close attention to pressing and the results will be stunning.

5. Layer a red 6"-long rectangle over the white rectangle, right sides together.

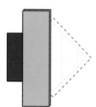

6. Carefully flip the pattern over while holding the white rectangle in place. Stitch on the line between areas 2 and 3, cut the threads, flip the pattern over again, open the red rectangle to the right side, and press well with your fingernail.

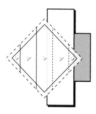

7. Continue in this manner to add fabric rectangles to the foundation pattern, alternating the colors. Use 3"-long rectangles for areas 1 and 5 and 6"-long rectangles for areas 2, 3, and 4.

8. After all of the areas have been covered, turn the pattern to the marked side and trim along the pattern outer edges. Gently remove the paper backing and press.

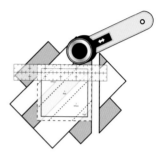

9. Repeat steps 2–8 to make a total of 60 blocks with a red stripe in the center.

Red striped block.
Make 60.

10. To make the white striped blocks, follow steps 2–8, reversing the colors so the white stripe is through the block center. Make 48.

White striped block.
Make 48.

ASSEMBLING THE RUNNER TOP

1. Alternately sew four red 3½" squares and three white striped blocks together, making sure all the stripes are angled correctly and running in the same direction. It's easy to turn them around! Press the seam allowances toward the red squares. Repeat to make a total of 16 rows.

Make 16.

2. Alternately sew four red striped blocks and three white 3½" squares together, again making sure the stripes are angled correctly and running in the same direction. Press the seam allowances toward the white squares. Repeat to make a total of 15 rows.

Make 15.

3. Refer to the runner assembly diagram below to alternately join the rows from steps 1 and 2. Press the seam allowances toward the rows with red squares.

4. Sew the red 2¾" x 93½" border strips to the sides of the runner top. Press the seam allowances toward the border strips. Add the red 2¾" x 26" strips to the top and bottom edges. Press the seam allowances toward the border strips.

Runner assembly

FINISHING

If you're making the bed runner reversible, refer to "Runner Flip Side: Suits Me!" (page 32) to make the flip side of the runner before proceeding. If you aren't making the bed runner reversible, use the backing fabric in place of the flip side in the following instructions.

1. Refer to "Making the Quilt Sandwich" (page 7) to layer the bed-runner top, batting, and flip side; baste the layers together.

2. Quilt as desired. In the runner shown, I used red thread to stitch in the ditch around the border. I quilted a straight line ¼" from the edge of the border, and then stippled in the channel that was created by that stitching line. I used white thread to stipple stitch the white areas, stitching over seam lines where white areas met to make the houndstooth units read as one.

3. Bind the edges using the dark gray 2½"-wide strips and a ⅜" seam allowance. Refer to "Binding" (page 7) as needed.

Runner Flip Side: Suits Me!

Unfinished Runner: 29½" x 108½"

MATERIALS

The flip side of the runner was made using yardage, but you could use recycled clothing if desired. Binding, backing, and batting yardages are given with the "Houndstooth Runner" materials list on page 29.

1¼ yards of 42"-wide white cotton pinpoint oxford fabric

⅝ yard of 58"-wide dark gray wool or wool-blend suiting fabric

⅝ yard of 58"-wide medium gray pinstriped wool or wool-blend suiting fabric

½ yard of 58"-wide light gray pinstriped wool or wool-blend suiting fabric

⅞ yard of 20"-wide lightweight fusible interfacing

4 red neckties*

One necktie can yield up to 4 strips, depending on the width of the tie; you'll need 13 strips.

CUTTING

From the dark gray suiting fabric, cut:

    1 rectangle, 6½" x 12½"

    1 rectangle, 5½" x 12½"

    6 rectangles, 4½" x 12½"

    3 rectangles, 3½" x 12½"

    3 rectangles, 2½" x 12½"

From the medium gray pinstriped suiting fabric, cut:

3 rectangles, 6½" x 12½"

2 rectangles, 5½" x 12½"

3 rectangles, 4½" x 12½"

8 rectangles, 3½" x 12½"

From the light gray pinstriped suiting fabric, cut:

2 rectangles, 6½" x 12½"

2 rectangles, 5½" x 12½"

2 rectangles, 4½" x 12½"

2 rectangles, 3½" x 12½"

2 rectangles, 2½" x 12½"

From the white pinpoint oxford fabric, cut:

2 rectangles, 6½" x 12½"

5 rectangles, 5½" x 12½"

9 rectangles, 4½" x 12½"

5 rectangles, 3½" x 12½"

3 rectangles, 2½" x 12½"

From the interfacing, cut:

13 strips, 2" x 13"

PREPARING THE NECKTIE STRIPS

1. Remove the stitching on the back of the neckties and open them up. Unstitch the lining and remove the interlining; discard the batting and lining. Press the ties flat using a low setting on your iron.

2. Follow the manufacturer's instructions to fuse the interfacing strips to the wrong side of the tie fabrics. Cut out each interfaced area and trim the strips to 1½" x 12½". Make 13.

ASSEMBLING AND FINISHING

1. Refer to the assembly diagram at right to arrange the suiting and oxford fabric rectangles into nine horizontal rows. Sew the rectangles in each row together. Press the seam allowances in alternate directions from row to row. Sew the rows together.

2. Refer to the finishing instructions for "Houndstooth Runner" (page 31) to layer, quilt, and bind the runner.

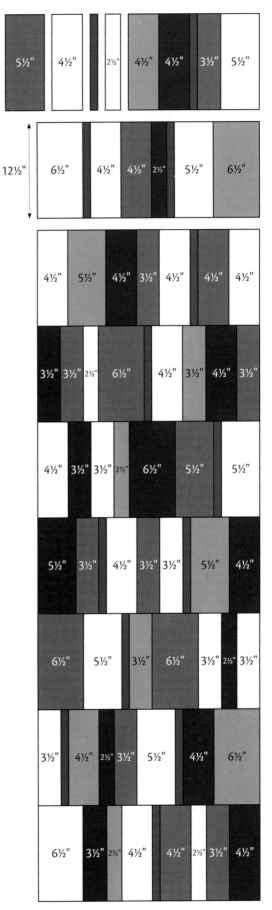

Runner assembly

Houndstooth Pillow

Finished Pillow: 14" x 32" • Finished Block: 3" x 3"

MATERIALS

Yardage is based on 42"-wide fabric unless otherwise noted.

⅞ yard of red solid for blocks and border

⅔ yard of 58"-wide dark gray wool or wool-blend suiting fabric for flip side and binding

⅜ yard of white solid for blocks

14" x 32" piece of plain cotton or muslin for front backing

14" x 32" piece of batting

⅛ yard of 20"-wide lightweight fusible interfacing

2 same-size buttons, ⅝" to 1¼" in diameter

13" x 31" pillow form *or* stuffing and ⅞ yard of plain cotton or muslin to make form

CUTTING

From the red solid, cut:
> 1 strip, 6" x 42"; crosscut into 18 rectangles, 1¾" x 6"
> 1 strip, 3" x 42"; crosscut into 16 rectangles, 1¾" x 3"
> 1 strip, 3½" x 42"; crosscut into 10 squares, 3½" x 3½"
> 2 strips, 2¾" x 27½"
> 2 strips, 2¾" x 14"

From the white solid, cut:
> 1 strip, 6" x 42"; crosscut into 21 rectangles, 1¾" x 6"
> 1 strip, 1¾" x 42"; crosscut into 10 rectangles, 1¾" x 3"
> 4 squares, 3½" x 3½"

From the dark gray suiting fabric, cut:
> 1 rectangle, 14" x 25½"
> 1 square, 14" x 14"
> 2 strips, 3⅛" x 58"

From the interfacing, cut:
> 2 strips, 1½" x 14"

MAKING THE PILLOW

1. Make 13 copies total of the foundation patterns (page 39): eight red striped and five white striped. Refer to "Making the Striped Blocks" (page 29) to make eight red striped squares and five white striped squares.

2. Sew a white striped block between two red solid squares. Press the seam allowances toward the red squares. Repeat to make a total of five rows.

Make 5 rows.

3. Sew a white solid square between two red striped blocks. Press the seam allowances toward the white squares. Repeat to make a total of four rows.

Make 4 rows.

4. Refer to the pillow assembly diagram below to alternately sew the rows together. Press the seam allowances toward the rows from step 2.

5. Sew the red solid 2¾" x 27½" border strips to the top and bottom of the pillow center. Press the seam allowances toward the strips. Sew the red solid 2¾" x 14" border strips to the sides of the pillow center. Press the seam allowances toward the strips.

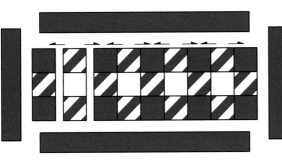

Pillow assembly

6. Layer the front backing piece, batting, and pieced top together; baste. Quilt, referring to the bed-runner quilting diagram (page 31), if desired.

7. Using the dark gray rectangle and square, refer to "Making the Flip Side" of "The Still Easy but Reversible Pillow" (page 13) to make the unquilted pillow back, making two buttonholes spaced 2" to each side of the center rather than three.

8. Stitch the pillow top to the pillow back, wrong sides together, using a scant ½" seam allowance. Bind the edges with the dark gray 3⅛"-wide strips using a ½" seam allowance.

9. Insert the pillow form into the cover. If you're making the pillow form, cut two rectangles, 15" x 33", from the plain cotton or muslin. Place the rectangles right sides together and sew around the edges using a ½" seam allowance. Leave a 6" opening along one long edge for turning. Turn the rectangle to the right side and firmly fill with stuffing. Sew the opening closed and insert the pillow form into the cover.

Boxed Shams with Cording

Finished Shams: 20" x 30" x 2"

MATERIALS
(for two standard-size shams)

Yardage is based on 42"-wide fabric unless otherwise noted.

3 yards of white solid for front and flip side

⅔ yard of 58"-wide gray pinstriped wool or wool-blend suiting fabric for flip side

¼ yard of red solid for front-side accent strip

1¼ yards of 58"-wide dark gray wool or wool-blend suiting fabric for cording

2 neckties*

13 yards of ⁸⁄₃₂"-diameter cording

⅔ yard of 20"-wide lightweight fusible interfacing

6 same-sized buttons, ⅝" to 1¼" in diameter

You may be able to get both shams from one tie, depending on the width of the tie.

CUTTING

From the white solid, cut:
 2 rectangles, 21" x 21¾" (A)
 2 rectangles, 12½" x 21" (B)
 4 strips, 2⅞" x 21"
 2 rectangles, 15¾" x 21" (C)
 2 rectangles, 9" x 21" (D)
 4 strips, 3" x 31"
 4 strips, 3" x 21"

From the red solid, cut:
 2 strips, 3" x 21"

From the gray pinstriped suiting fabric, cut:
 2 rectangles, 7¾" x 21"

From the dark gray suiting fabric, cut:
 Enough 1¾"-wide bias strips to yield a 440" strip after piecing

From the interfacing, cut:
 4 strips, 2" x 21"
 2 strips, 4" x 22"

MAKING THE BUTTONED FRONT SIDES

1. To make the buttonhole band for the front side (pictured on page 34), fuse an interfacing 2" x 21" strip to the wrong side of a white 2⅞" x 21" strip, ½" from one edge.

2. Fold a red strip in half lengthwise, wrong sides together, and press. Layer the red strip between one interfaced and one non-interfaced white 2⅞" strip, right sides together with the raw edges aligned. Sew using a ½" seam allowance. Turn right sides out and press.

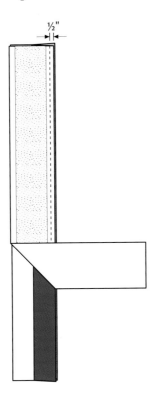

3. Align the buttonhole band with the 21" side of an A rectangle, right sides together and raw edges aligned. Sew using a ⅜" seam allowance. Press the seam allowances toward the rectangle. Flip the button band onto the rectangle, snugging the seam-allowance raw edges into the new fold. Stitch in the ditch of the seam

line to enclose the seam allowances. Flip the button band back to the right side and press the enclosed seam allowances toward the rectangle.

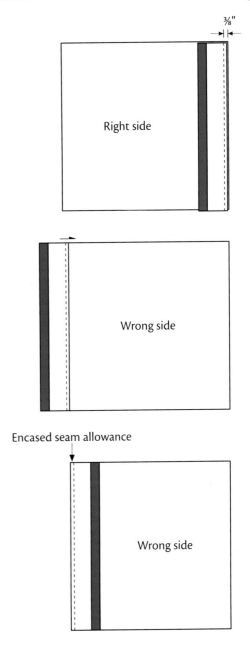

Right side

Wrong side

Encased seam allowance

Wrong side

4. Make three vertical buttonholes in the band, one in the center and one 6" on each side of the center.

5. To make the button band, fuse an interfacing 2" x 21" strip to the wrong side of a B rectangle along the 21" side, aligning the edges. Fold the interfaced edge to the wrong side twice and stitch along the first folded edge.

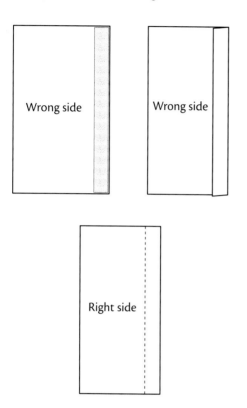

6. Repeat steps 1–5 to make a total of two sham fronts.

MAKING THE FLIP SIDES

1. Refer to "Preparing the Necktie Strips" (page 33) to take apart one necktie. Fuse the interfacing 4" x 22" strip to the wrong side of the prepared fabric and cut a 3" x 21" strip from the interfaced piece.

2. Fold the necktie strip in half lengthwise, wrong sides together, and press. Layer the necktie strip between the pinstriped rectangle and rectangle D, right sides together with the raw edges aligned. Sew using a ½" seam allowance. Turn

and press. Topstitch the edge of the pinstriped fabric closest to the necktie strip.

3. Sew a C rectangle to the raw edge of the pinstriped fabric.

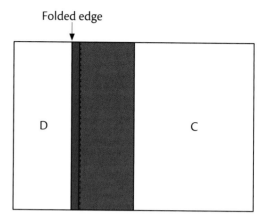

4. Repeat steps 1–4 to make a total of two flip sides.

ASSEMBLING THE SHAMS

1. Cover the cord using the 1¾"-wide dark gray strips. Refer to "Making Piping" (page 9) as needed.

2. To ensure that the flip side and the front side are the same size, place a flip side right side up on your work surface. Lay one set of front pieces over the flip side, right sides together with the raw edges on the short ends aligned and the button band over the buttonhole band. Pin the ends of the button/buttonhole bands together, but not to the flip side. Do not stitch the front to the flip side.

3. Using a zipper foot and a ½" seam allowance, attach the piping to the right side of the front side and flip-side pieces, aligning the raw edges. Snug the foot as close to the cord as possible when sewing.

4. To make the box band, join two white 3" x 21" strips and two white 3" x 31" strips end to end to make a circle, alternating the strip lengths.

5. Pin the box band to the sham flip side, aligning the raw edges and matching the band seams to the sham corners. Using a zipper foot, stitch the band in place, snugging the foot against the cording.

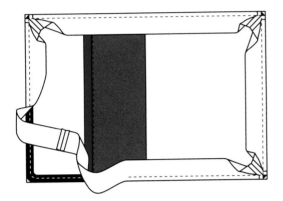

6. Align the remaining raw edge of the box band with the front piece in the same manner, making sure the sham right sides are together and the red strips on each side are aligned; sew.

7. Serge or zigzag over the seam allowances, clip the corners, and turn the sham to the right side. Sew the buttons to the button band to correspond to the buttonholes.

8. Repeat steps 1–8 to make a total of two shams.

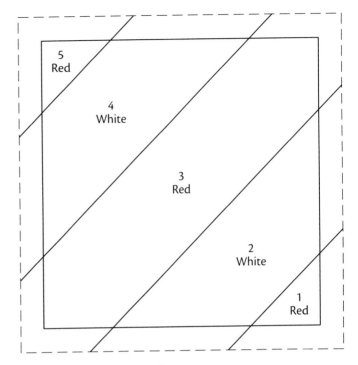

Foundation pattern
Red striped block

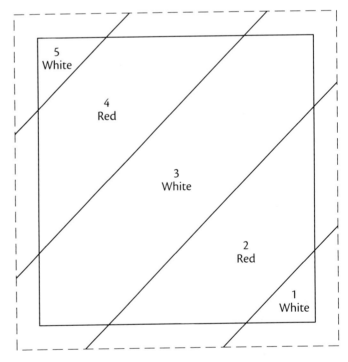

Foundation pattern
White striped block

Make Your Bed
SASSY

Indecision inspired this fanciful ensemble. My daughter couldn't decide what color she wanted her room to be, so we decided to appliqué circles of her favorite colors onto a black-and-white background. When she wants to add more colors, she can change the button-on splotches to suit her mood.

Pizzazz Runner

Finished Runner: 24½" x 70½", including 3" detachable fringed bands • Finished Block: 8" x 8"

MATERIALS

8 fat quarters of assorted white-on-black prints

8 fat quarters of assorted black-on-white prints

5 fat eighths of bright fabrics for button-on splotches (these can be different colors or all from the same color family)

Scraps, approximately 7" to 12" square *each*, of assorted bright-colored fabrics in hot pink, yellow, lime green, aqua, and blue for appliquéd circles and fringed band

¼ yard *each* of two different bright-colored fabrics for binding

2⅛ yards of fabric for backing (only needed if not using the pieced flip side)

30" x 70" piece of batting

1½ yards of 20"-wide lightweight fusible interfacing

Template plastic

22 buttons, ¾" diameter: 10 white for splotches; 3 *each* of yellow, green, pink, and blue for fringed band

1½ yards of beaded fringe

CUTTING

Before you begin, use your favorite appliqué method to create circle templates in a variety of sizes from 4½" to 10" in diameter using a compass or circular objects around your house to trace around.

From *each* of the 8 assorted white-on-black prints, cut:
  1 square, 8½" x 8½" (8 total)
  1 strip, 9" x 21" (8 total); crosscut into strips,
    9" x random widths from 1½" to 3"

From *each* of the 8 assorted black-on-white prints, cut:
  1 square, 8½" x 8½" (8 total)
  1 strip, 9" x 21" (8 total); crosscut into strips,
    9" x random widths from 1½" to 3"

From the assorted bright-colored scraps, cut a *total* of:
  18 to 20 circles in various sizes
  32 rectangles, 2" x 7"

From the interfacing, cut:
  2 strips, 3" x 24"
  5 rectangles, 8" x 16"

From *each* of the 2 binding fabrics, cut:
  2 strips, 2½" x 42" (4 total)

ASSEMBLING THE RUNNER TOP

1. Randomly select white-on-black and black-on-white 9"-long strips and sew them together to equal a piece approximately 9" wide. Press the seam allowances in one direction. Trim the piece to 8½" x 8½". Repeat to make a total of eight blocks.

Make 8.

2. Randomly arrange the pieced blocks from step 1 and the white-on-black and black-on-white 8½" squares into eight rows of three blocks each. Rotate the pieced blocks so some strips run vertically and some run horizontally. Stitch the blocks in each row together. Press the seam allowances in alternate directions from row to row. Sew the rows together. Press the seam allowances as desired.

3. Arrange the circles on the quilt top as desired. Layer some circles over each other and run others partially off the edge. When you're happy with the placement, appliqué the circles in place by hand or machine using your favorite method.

Trim the circles that extend past the edge even with the base. If you used a non-fusible method, turn the runner to the wrong side and trim away the base fabric behind each appliqué, leaving a ¼" seam allowance.

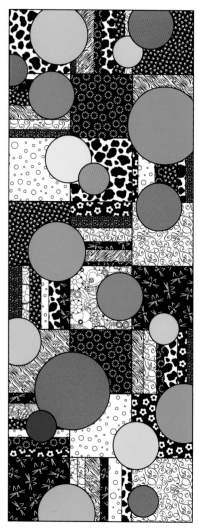

Runner assembly

MAKING THE SPLOTCHES

1. Center an interfacing 8" x 16" rectangle on the wrong side of each fat eighth and fuse it in place, following the manufacturer's instructions. Trace the splotch pattern (page 50) onto template plastic and cut it out. Use the template to cut two splotches from each interfaced fat eighth.

2. With right sides together, stitch around the edges of the interfaced splotches using a ¼" seam allowance and leaving an opening on one edge of each splotch as shown for turning. Clip the seam allowances liberally. Turn the splotches

right side out using the eraser end of a pencil to push the "fingers" through the opening and smooth out the curves. Hand stitch the opening closed.

3. Make a ¾"-long buttonhole in the center of each splotch.

MAKING THE FRINGED BANDS

1. Arrange 16 bright-colored 2" x 7" rectangles side by side, alternating the colors. Sew the rectangles together along the long edges. Repeat to make a total of two strips.

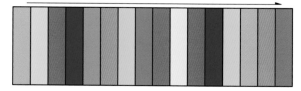

Make 2.

2. Fold each band in half lengthwise, right sides together, and press. Unfold the bands. Center and fuse an interfacing 3" x 24" strip to the wrong side of one half of the band.

3. Turn the bands to the right side. Cut the beaded fringe in half to make two equal pieces. Place one length of fringe on each pieced band so that the bottom edge of the fringe lip is aligned with the fold line of the band. Stitch through the lip of each fringe length to secure it to the band.

Crease →

4. Fold each band right sides together, making sure the fringe is tucked inside. Stitch along the raw edges using a ½" seam allowance and leaving an opening for turning along the long edge of each band. Turn the bands right side out and hand stitch the opening closed.

Fold

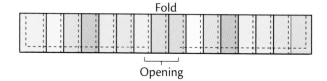

Opening

42

5. Make ¾"-long vertical buttonholes ¼" from the seamed edge of the band, placing one on each end rectangle and then every third rectangle.

FINISHING

If you're making the bed runner reversible, refer to "Runner Flip Side: Starry Night" (page 46) to make the flip side of the runner before proceeding. If you're not making the bed runner reversible, use the backing fabric in place of the flip side in the following instructions.

1. Refer to "Making the Quilt Sandwich" (page 7) to layer the bed-runner top, batting, and flip side.

2. Quilt the layers together. In the runner shown, I began the quilting with four "ribbons" that stretch across the bed runner, one each in blue, green, pink, and yellow. Then I filled the ribbons with different infill patterns, such as swirls, squiggles, and waves. After quilting, trim the batting and flip side even with the runner top.

3. Sew the 2½"-wide binding strips of each color together, and then sew those strips together to make one long strip. Bind the edges using a ⅜" seam allowance. Refer to "Binding" (page 7) as needed.

4. Sew the colored buttons on the runner ends to correspond to the fringe band using a button that's a different color than the rectangle it will be attached to. Mark the button location on the runner front and back where desired for each splotch. Sew the buttons in place. Button the splotches to the front or back as desired.

Pizzazz Pillow

Finished Pillow: 21½" x 21½"

MATERIALS

Yardage is based on 42"-wide fabric unless otherwise noted.

¾ yard of fabric for pillow back (only needed if not using the pieced flip side)

4 rectangles, 9" x 10", of white-on-black print

4 rectangles, 9" x 10", of black-on-white print

Scraps, approximately 6" to 9" square *each*, of assorted bright-colored fabrics in hot pink, yellow, lime green, aqua, and blue for circle appliqués and border

1 fat eighth of bright-colored fabric for splotch

⅜ yard of black fabric for binding

26" x 26" piece of plain cotton or muslin for front lining

26" x 26" piece of batting

⅓ yard of 20"-wide lightweight fusible interfacing

Template plastic

1 white ¾"-diameter button

14" x 14" square pillow form

CUTTING

Before you begin, use your favorite appliqué method to create circle templates in a variety of sizes from 4½" to 10" in diameter using a compass or circular objects around your house to trace around.

From *each* of the 4 white-on-black prints, cut:
1 square, 4¼" x 4¼" (4 total)
2 strips, 9" x random widths from 1½" to 3" (8 total)

From *each* of the 4 black-on-white prints, cut:
1 square, 4¼" x 4¼" (4 total)
2 strips, 9" x random widths from 1½" to 3" (8 total)

From the assorted bright-colored scraps, cut a *total* of:
5 circles in various sizes
48 rectangles, 2" x 3½"

From the interfacing, cut:
1 rectangle, 8" x 16"

From the black fabric for binding, cut:
3 strips, 3⅛" x 42"

MAKING THE PILLOW

1. Randomly select white-on-black and black-on-white 9"-long strips and sew them together to equal a piece approximately 9" wide. Press the seam allowances in one direction. Trim the piece to 8" x 8". Repeat to make a total of two striped units.

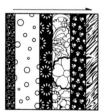

Make 2.

2. Sew each black-on-white square to a white-on-black square to make four pairs. Press the seam allowances toward the white-on-black squares. Sew two pairs together, alternating the fabrics to make a checkerboard unit. Press the seam allowances in either direction. Repeat to make a total of two units.

Make 2.

3. Arrange the units into two vertical rows of two blocks each as shown. Sew the units in each row together. Press the seam allowances toward the checkerboard units. Sew the rows together to complete the pillow center. Press the seam allowances in either direction.

4. Refer to the photo (page 43) as needed to arrange the circles on the pillow center and stitch them in place using your favorite appliqué method. Trim any circles that overlap the edges even with the pillow center.

5. Randomly join 12 bright-colored 2" x 3½" rectangles along their long edges to make a border strip. Repeat to make a total of four border strips. Sew the first border strip to the

pillow top, stopping 2" from the corner. Working clockwise around the pillow center, add a border strip to each side, pressing the seam allowances toward the border after each addition. After the fourth strip has been added, finish sewing the first strip in place.

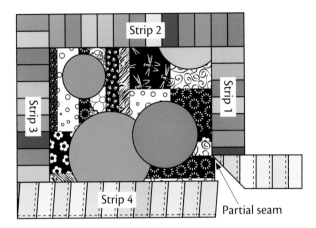

Zebra Sheet and Pillowcases

FINISHING

If you're making the pillow reversible, refer to "Pillow Flip Side: Starry Night" (page 48) to make the flip side of the pillow before proceeding. If you're not making the pillow reversible, use the back fabric in place of the flip side in the following instructions.

1. Refer to "Making the Quilt Sandwich" (page 7) to layer the front lining piece, batting, and pieced top; baste the layers together. Quilt, referring to the photo (page 43) if desired.

2. Refer to "Assembling the Pillow" (page 14) to align the edges of the pillow top and flip side, wrong sides together. Stitch the pieces together using a scant ½" seam allowance. Bind the edges with the black 3⅛"-wide strips using a ½" seam allowance.

3. From the front side, stitch in the ditch of the border seam to make the 3" flange.

4. Refer to "Making the Splotches" (page 42) to make one splotch from the bright-colored fat eighth. Sew the button to the pillow front where desired. Attach the splotch to the button.

5. Insert the pillow form into the cover.

Refer to "Adding a Fabric Band to a Flat Sheet" (page 11) and "Making a Pillowcase with a Fabric Band" (page 12) to make the sheet and the desired number of pillowcases.

Runner Flip Side: Starry Night

Unfinished Runner: 28½" x 64½"

MATERIALS

Yardage is based on 42"-wide fabric. Binding, backing, and batting yardages are given with the "Pizzazz Runner" materials list on page 41.

½ yard *each* of green, purple, medium blue, and hot pink prints for background

⅜ yard of orange print for background

⅓ yard of white print for stars

⅓ yard of light blue print for background

¼ yard of yellow print for background

CUTTING

From the white print, cut:
   3 squares, 2½" x 2½"
   12 rectangles, 3" x 8"

From the green print, cut:
   2 rectangles, 6½" x 18½"
   2 rectangles, 6½" x 8½"
   1 rectangle, 2½" x 18½"
   1 rectangle, 2½" x 8½"
   2 rectangles, 2½" x 6½"

From the purple print, cut:
1 rectangle, 6½" x 16½"
1 rectangle, 6½" x 10½"
1 rectangle, 4½" x 16½"
1 rectangle, 4½" x 10½"
1 rectangle, 2½" x 16½"
1 rectangle, 2½" x 10½"
1 rectangle, 2½" x 6½"
1 rectangle, 2½" x 4½"

From the medium blue print, cut:
1 rectangle, 10½" x 14½"
1 rectangle, 10½" x 12½"
1 rectangle, 2½" x 10½"

From the hot pink print, cut:
2 rectangles, 6½" x 28½"

From the orange print, cut:
1 rectangle, 10½" x 28½"

From the light blue print, cut:
1 rectangle, 6½" x 14½"
1 rectangle, 6½" x 12½"
1 rectangle, 2½" x 14½"
1 rectangle, 2½" x 12½"
1 rectangle, 2½" x 6½"

From the yellow print, cut:
1 rectangle, 4½" x 28½"

MAKING THE STAR RAYS

1. Fold the green, purple, medium blue, and light blue 2½"-wide background rectangles in half lengthwise to mark the centerline on each piece.

2. Lay a background rectangle right side up. Place a white 3" x 8" rectangle right side down over the background rectangle, lining up the long edge with the centerline and a random point along the long edge of the background rectangle. Stitch ¼" from the long edge of the white rectangle.

Centerline

3. Fold the white fabric to the right side and press the seam allowances toward the white fabric with an iron or your fingernail. Flip the unit over and trim the white fabric even with the edges of the background rectangle. Save the leftover scrap of white fabric for the next ray.

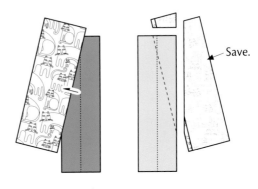

Save.

4. Turn the unit to the right side. Fold the white fabric back and trim the seam allowances to ¼".

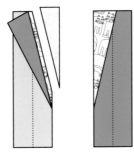

5. Using the leftover piece from the white rectangle, repeat steps 2–4 on the opposite side of the same end of the piece from step 3.

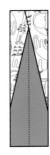

6. Repeat steps 2–5 for the remaining background pieces to make a total of 12 star-ray units.

ASSEMBLING AND FINISHING

1. Refer to the assembly diagram to lay out the star units and the remaining pieces into horizontal rows. Sew the pieces in each row together. Press the seam allowances away from the star units. Sew the rows together. Press the seam allowances as desired.

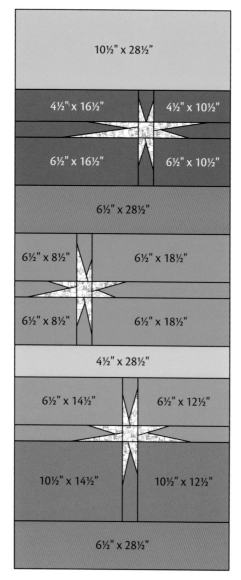

Runner assembly

2. Refer to the finishing instructions for "Pizzazz Runner" (page 43) to layer, quilt, and bind the runner.

Pillow Flip Side: Starry Night

Finished Pillow: 21½" x 21½"

MATERIALS

Yardage is based on 42"-wide fabric unless otherwise noted.

¾ yard of blue fabric for background

⅛ yard of white fabric for star

18" x 22" piece of plain cotton or muslin for backing

⅛ yard of 20"-wide lightweight fusible interfacing

3 white ¾"-diameter buttons

CUTTING

From the blue fabric, cut:
    1 rectangle, 2½" x 7¾"
    1 rectangle, 2½" x 7¼"
    1 rectangle, 2½" x 11¼"
    1 rectangle, 2½" x 12¾"
    1 rectangle, 7¼" x 7¾" (A)
    1 rectangle, 7¾" x 12¾" (B)
    1 rectangle, 7¼" x 11¼" (C)
    1 rectangle, 11¼" x 12¾" (D)
    1 rectangle, 9" x 21½" (E)

From the white fabric, cut:
    1 square, 2½" x 2½"
    4 rectangles, 3" x 8"

From the interfacing, cut:
    2 strips, 1½" x 21"

48

MAKING THE PILLOW FLIP SIDE

1. Refer to "Making the Star Rays" (page 47) to make four star rays using the blue 2½"-wide rectangles and the white rectangles.

2. Arrange the star rays, the white 2" square, and blue rectangles A–D into three vertical rows as shown. Sew the pieces in each row together. Press the seam allowances toward the rectangles and white square. Sew the rows together. Press the seam allowances away from the center row.

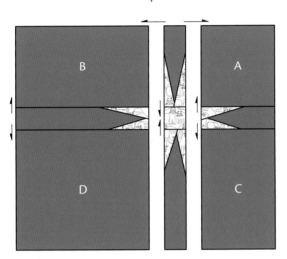

3. To make the buttonhole band, fuse a strip of interfacing to the wrong side of the 21" edge farthest from the star. Turn the edge under 1½" twice. Unfold the band once and lay the backing fabric on the wrong side of the flip side so one long edge is snugged into the fold. Refold the band over the backing and baste around the raw edges. Stitch across the band close to the first fold. Trim the backing even with the flip-side edges. Make three buttonholes in the band, one in the center and one 4" from each side of the center.

4. To make the button band, fuse a strip of interfacing to the long edge of rectangle E. Turn under the interfaced edge 1½" twice and stitch close to the first fold. Layer the buttonhole band over the button band and baste the ends together. Sew the buttons to the button band to correspond to the buttonholes.

5. Refer to "Finishing" (page 45) to finish the pillow.

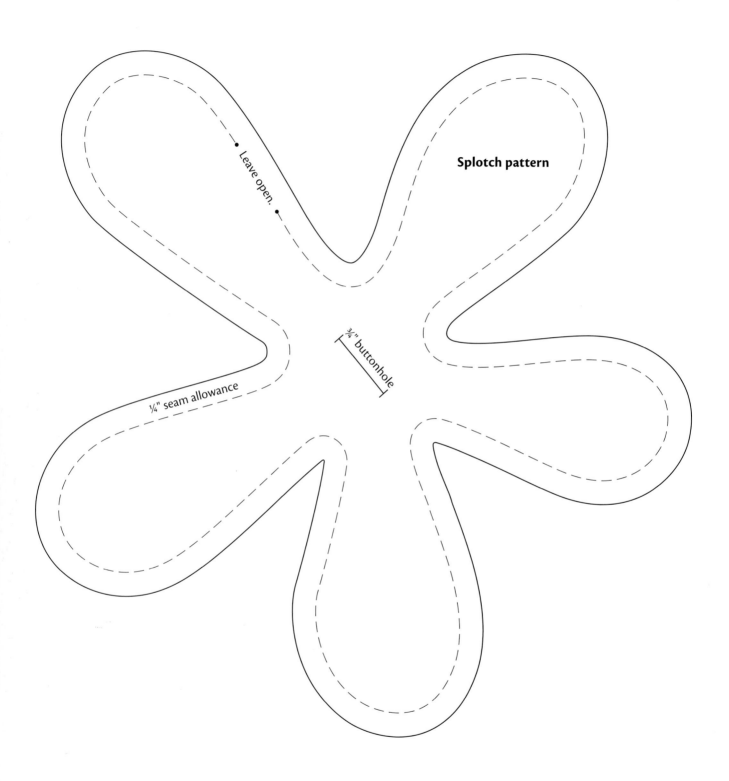

Splotch pattern

Leave open.

¾" buttonhole

¼" seam allowance

Make Your Bed
SERENE

Beautiful batiks in teals, blues, and purples cover this bed in calming serenity. Metallic thread and crystals add light and sparkle to the soft, curvy feather quilting. Try a solid backing with contrasting thread that will show off the quilting on the flip side.

Waves Runner

Finished Runner: 105½" x 26½" • Finished Block: 17½ x 25½

MATERIALS

Yardage is based on 42"-wide fabric.

⅔ yard *each or* 20" x 30" rectangle *each* of 6 assorted fabrics for blocks*

¾ yard of dark blue fabric for binding

3¼ yards of fabric for backing

32" x 111" piece of batting

20" x 30" piece of paper (optional)

Silver metallic thread for quilting (optional)

720 sapphire size SS16 (4.0 mm) hot-fix flat-back crystal rhinestones and applicator (optional)

Chalk marker

* See "Be Creative!" below for fabric options.

Be Creative!

The six 20" x 30" fabric rectangles can each be cut from a different single fabric, or they can be pieced from random-sized strips to make pieces of fabric that measure 20" x 30". The runner shown used two pieces that were made from three 9½" x 30" strips of fabric arranged from light to dark. You can be as creative as you like! As long as the fabric pieces are 20" x 30", anything will work!

CUTTING

From *each* of the 6 assorted fabrics, cut:
    1 rectangle, 20" x 30" (6 total)

From the dark blue fabric, cut:
    Enough 2½"-wide bias strips to yield a 270" strip after piecing

MAKING THE PATTERN

Enlarge the Waves Runner block pattern (page 56) 333%. You can do this at your local copy shop or use a grid to transfer the curves to a 20" x 30" piece of paper. Better yet, make your pattern unique by drawing your own gentle curves onto the paper.

CUTTING THE CURVES

1. Stack all six fabric rectangles in the order you wish them to appear. For this runner, the fabrics were stacked teal, dark blue, medium blue, pieced purple, purple, and pieced blue. It doesn't matter if you start your order on the top or bottom of the stack.

2. Center the pattern over the stack, pin through the layers of each segment, and then cut along the curved lines. Keep the stacks stacked and in order, but remove the pattern.

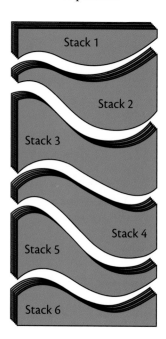

3. Leave the first stack in the order cut. From the second stack, take the top piece and place it on the bottom of the stack. From the third stack, take the top two pieces and place them on the bottom of the stack. Continue in this manner, taking three pieces from the fourth stack and four pieces from the fifth stack and placing them on the bottom of the stacks. From the sixth stack, take the bottom piece and place it on top of the stack.

Curvy Tips

It's easier to sew curves with the inside curve on the top, so stop, cut the threads, and sew from the other side when the curve changes.

Perfection is not required! Use the marks as guidelines and ease in the fabric where it wants to be.

Pin, pin, pin! Remove your pins before your needle hits them to avoid puckers and broken needles.

Press seam allowances toward the outside curve. When the curve changes, clip the seam allowances almost to the stitching and flip the seam allowances the other way, toward the new outside curve. The natural stretch in the fabric allows the curves to lie flat when pressed.

ASSEMBLING THE RUNNER

1. Take the top layer of each stack and lay out the block with the curved edges just touching. Mark a chalk line across the ¼" seam allowances as registration marks for sewing. Clip the inside curves about ⅛" deep.

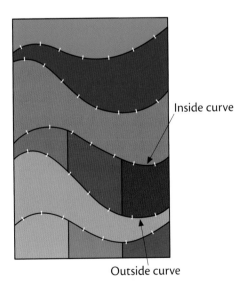

Inside curve

Outside curve

2. Pin and sew the curved pieces together with a ¼" seam allowance, matching the marks and easing the seams.

3. Repeat steps 1 and 2 for the remaining layers to make a total of six blocks.

4. Trim the blocks to 18" x 26". Arrange them as desired. Stitch the blocks together and press the seam allowances to one side.

FINISHING

1. Refer to "Making the Quilt Sandwich" (page 7) to layer the bed-runner top, batting, and backing; baste the layers together.

2. Quilt as desired. I drew four wavy lines across the runner with chalk, spacing them at least 2" apart. After quilting the wavy lines I filled in the space between the lines with a feather pattern. After quilting, trim the batting and backing even with the runner top. Curve the corners using a plate or cup as a template.

3. Bind the edges using the dark blue 2½"-wide bias strips and a ⅜" seam allowance. Refer to "Binding" (page 7) as needed.

4. Add the crystal rhinestones, if desired, following the instructions for your applicator. Space the crystals about ¾" apart along the spines of the quilted feathers. Your quilt may require more or fewer crystals than specified based on the number of feathers you quilt. Just remember, there is no such thing as too much sparkle!

Waves Pillow

Finished Pillow: 21" x 21"

MATERIALS

Yardage is based on 42"-wide fabric unless otherwise noted.

¾ yard *each* of 3 assorted fabrics for front and flip side

⅓ yard of fabric for binding

1⅝ yards of plain cotton or muslin for lining

26" x 52" piece of batting

⅛ yard of 20"-wide lightweight fusible interfacing

23" x 23" piece of paper (optional)

3 same-sized buttons, ⅝" to ¾" in diameter

160 sapphire size SS16 (4.0 mm) hot-fix flat-back crystal rhinestones and applicator (optional)

20" x 20" pillow form

CUTTING

From *each* of the 3 front and flip-side fabrics, cut:
    1 square, 23" x 23" (3 total)

From the interfacing, cut:
    2 strips, 1½" x 20"

From *each* of the backing fabric and batting, cut:
    2 squares, 26" x 26"

From the binding fabric, cut:
    3 strips, 3⅛" x 42"

MAKING THE BLOCKS

1. Prepare the paper pattern, referring to "Making the Pattern" (page 52) and enlarging the Waves Pillow block pattern (page 57) 400%, or make your own pattern.
2. Refer to "Cutting the Curves" (page 52) to layer the fabrics and cut them into three stacks.

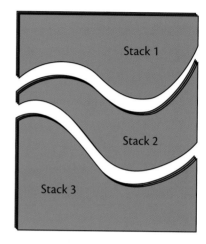

3. Follow steps 1–3 of "Assembling the Runner" (page 53) to make three blocks. One block will be for the pillow front and another block will be used for the pillow flip side. The third block will not be used. Set it aside for another project, or consider making another pillow with a plain back.
4. Refer to "Making the Quilt Sandwich" (page 7) to layer a lining square, batting square, and block; baste the layers together. Repeat to make a total of two basted blocks. Quilt the blocks to match the runner (page 53), if desired.

ASSEMBLING AND FINISHING

1. Trim the quilted blocks to 21" x 21".
2. To make the button band and buttonhole band, cut a 21" x 4" strip from the remainder of both the bottom wave fabrics. Fold each 21" x 4" strip in half lengthwise, wrong sides together. Open up each strip and fuse an interfacing strip to the wrong side of one half of the strip, butting the interfacing long edge against the fold line and leaving ½" of fabric exposed along the opposite raw edge. Refold the bands in half.

3. With right sides together, sew a matching band to the bottom edge of the flip-side block using a ½" seam allowance. Press the band to the wrong side of the block. Make a horizontal buttonhole at the center of the band and 6" on each side of the center, stitching through all of the layers.

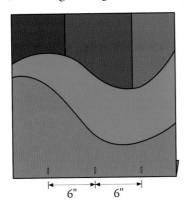

4. With the raw edges aligned, place the remaining band (which will have the buttons on it) along the bottom edge of the wrong side of the pillow front; baste across the long edge only. Layer the flip side and front wrong sides together, aligning the top and side edges. The button band will extend ½" below the buttonhole band. Using a scant ½" seam allowance, stitch around all four sides of the pillow, making sure not to catch the buttonhole band in the stitching.

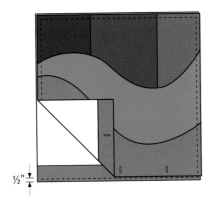

5. Bind the edges with the binding strips using a ½" seam allowance and again making sure not to catch the button band in the binding. Refer to "Binding" (page 7) as needed.

6. On the inside of the pillow, sew the buttons to the button band to correspond to the buttonhole locations.

7. Add the crystal rhinestones, if desired, following the instructions for your applicator.

8. Insert the pillow form into the cover.

Waves Shams and Fringed Pillows

Refer to "Shams: The Same but Different!" (page 15) and "The Easiest Pillow Ever" (page 13) for materials and instructions to make the shams and pillows. Each side of the pillows and shams is made of different batiks. Take this opportunity to show off all the gorgeous batiks you just couldn't pass up!

Waves Runner block pattern
Enlarge 333%.
Actual size: 20" x 30"

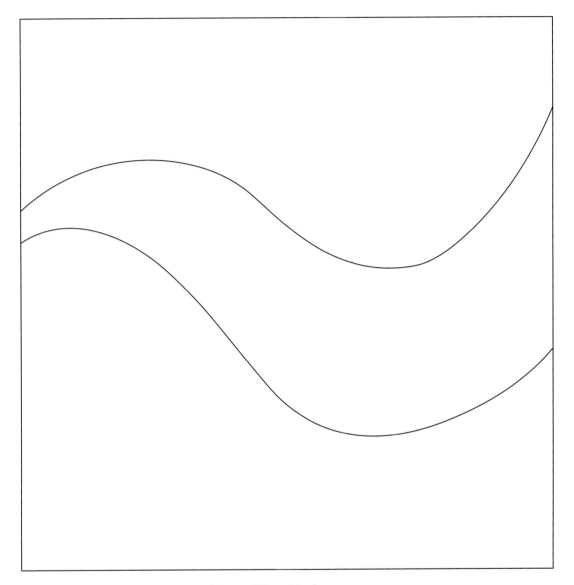

Waves Pillow block pattern
Enlarge 400%.
Actual size: 23" x 23"

Make Your Bed
PLAYFUL

There's lots of room for artistic interpretation in this design. For the pieced blocks, I used odds and ends of bright-colored fabrics from my scrap bag. If you don't have scraps, an assortment of fat eighths or fat quarters will work just fine. If you don't like the colors I used, pick ones that work for you. And if you get tired of piecing 3" blocks, substitute plain squares!

Tiny Squares Runner

Finished Runner: 27½" x 93½" • Finished Blocks: 3" x 3" and 6" x 6"

MATERIALS

Yardage is based on 42"-wide fabric.

3 yards *total* of assorted bright-colored fabrics for blocks

1 yard of white fabric for blocks and binding

3 yards of fabric for backing

30" x 100" piece of batting

CUTTING

Cut pieces for each set from the same fabric.

From the assorted bright-colored fabrics, cut:

15 sets of 2 rectangles, 2½" x 6½", and 2 squares, 2½" x 2½" (for 6" blocks)

139 sets of 2 rectangles, 1½" x 3½", and 2 squares, 1½" x 1½" (for 3" blocks)

40 squares, 3½" x 3½"

From the white fabric, cut:

6 strips, 1½" x 42"; crosscut into 139 squares, 1½" x 1½"

1 strip, 2½" x 42"; crosscut into 15 squares, 2½" x 2½"

7 strips, 2¼" x 42"

MAKING THE BLOCKS

1. Using one set of pieces cut for the 6" blocks, sew 2½" squares to opposite sides of a white 2½" square. Press the seam allowances away from the white square. Sew the rectangles to the sides of this unit. Press the seam allowances toward the rectangles. Repeat to make a total of 15 blocks.

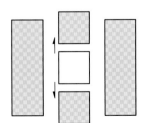 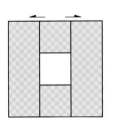

Make 15.

2. Repeat step 1 with the sets cut for the 3" blocks and the white 1½" squares to make 139 blocks.

Make 139.

ASSEMBLING AND FINISHING

1. Refer to the assembly diagram (page 60) to lay out the blocks and bright-colored 3½" squares. Rearrange pieced blocks and squares as desired. Note that the outer seams of the pieced blocks alternate horizontally and vertically so you never have to match seams. When you're happy with the layout, take a picture for reference or label all the blocks by row and column. It's very easy to get mixed up.

2. Sew the blocks and squares into smaller sections as shown, and then sew the bigger sections into rows. Press the seam allowances in opposite directions from row to row to allow them to match up nicely. The seam allowances of any block that "sticks out" at the ends should be pressed toward the block that sticks out. Sew the rows together. Press the seam allowances as desired.

3. Refer to "Making the Quilt Sandwich" (page 7) to layer the bed-runner top, batting, and backing; baste the layers together.

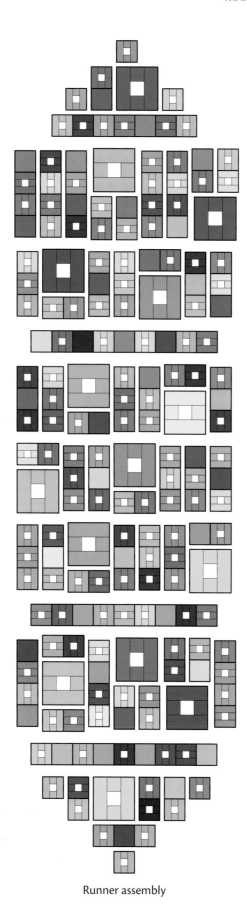

4. Quilt as desired. The runner shown was quilted with wiggly lines across the quilt. I also quilted some square motifs, making sure the corners of the quilted squares lined up with the center of a block and going over the stitching twice to give the motifs extra weight. After quilting, trim the batting and backing even with the runner top.

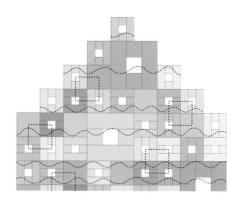

5. Bind the edges using the white 2¼"-wide strips and a ¼" seam allowance. Refer to "Binding" (page 7) as needed.

Runner assembly

Tiny Squares Shams

Finished Shams: 26" x 32"

MATERIALS

(for two standard-size shams)

Yardage is based on 42"-wide fabric unless otherwise noted.

3¾ yards of white fabric for front, flip side, and binding

1 yard *total* of assorted bright-colored fabrics for blocks

1¾ yards of fabric for front lining

⅞ yard of 20"-wide lightweight fusible interfacing

6 buttons, ⅝" to 1¼" diameter

Note: The front of the shams shown are lined and quilted, but they do not have a batting layer.

CUTTING

Cut pieces for each set from the same fabric.

From the assorted bright-colored fabrics, cut:
    36 sets of 2 rectangles, 1½" x 3½", and 2 squares, 1½" x 1½"
    12 squares, 3½" x 3½"

From the white fabric, cut:
    2 strips, 1½" x 42"; crosscut into 36 squares, 1½" x 1½"
    2 rectangles, 12½" x 18½"
    2 squares, 26" x 26"
    2 rectangles, 15" x 26"
    4 strips, 4¼" x 24½"
    4 strips, 4¼" x 26"
    7 strips, 3⅛" x 42"

From the interfacing, cut:
    2 strips, 1½" x 26"

From the backing fabric, cut:
    2 rectangles, 28" x 34"

MAKING THE SHAMS

1. Refer to step 2 of "Making the Blocks" (page 59) to make 36 pieced 3" blocks.
2. Refer to the sham assembly diagram to arrange 18 blocks and six 3½" bright-colored squares around a white 12½" x 18½" rectangle. Note that the outer seams of the pieced blocks alternate horizontally and vertically so you never have to match seams. Sew the pieces along the top and bottom together in the order determined. Join these strips to the top and bottom of the white rectangle. Press the seam allowances toward the block strips. Make the side strips in the same manner. Sew the strips to the sides of the white rectangle. Press the seam allowances toward the block strips.
3. Sew the white 4¼" x 24½" strips to the top and bottom of the sham center. Press the seam allowances toward the blocks. Add the white 4¼" x 26" strips to the sides of the sham center.
4. Layer the backing and sham top, wrong sides together, and stay stitch around the edges. Stitch in the ditch of each block.

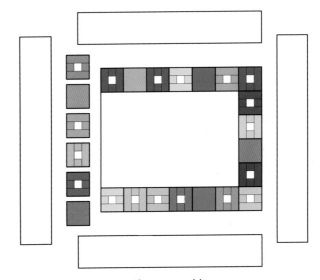

Sham assembly

5. Refer to "Making the Sham" (page 15) to finish the sham using "The Still Easy but Reversible Sham" instructions. Bind the edges using the white 3⅛"-wide strips and a ½" seam allowance.
6. Repeat steps 2–5 to make a total of two shams.

Not-So-Tiny Square Pillow

Finished Pillow: 17" x 17"

MATERIALS

Yardage is based on 42"-wide fabric.

⅜ yard of white fabric for front and flip side

⅓ yard of blue fabric for flip side

⅛ yard of 20"-wide lightweight fusible interfacing

2 same-sized buttons, ⅝" to 1¼" in diameter

16" x 16" square pillow form

CUTTING

From the white fabric, cut:
    1 rectangle, 6½" x 9¼"
    2 strips, 1¾" x 17"
    2 strips, 1¾" x 13¼"
    2 strips, 1¾" x 8¾"
    2 strips, 3⅛" x 42"
    1 square, 17" x 17"

From the blue fabric, cut:
    1 rectangle, 8¾" x 14½"
    1 rectangle, 4½" x 14½"
    2 rectangles, 4½" x 9¼"

From the interfacing, cut:
    2 strips, 1½" x 17"

MAKING THE PILLOW

1. To make the buttoned half of the flip side, sew white 1¾" x 8¾" strips to the top and bottom of the blue 8¾" x 14½" rectangle. Press the seam allowances toward the blue rectangle. Add a white 1¾" x 17" strip to the long right edge of the blue rectangle. Press the seam allowance toward the blue rectangle. Fuse an interfacing strip to the wrong side of the long left edge and fold it under 1½" twice. Stitch close to the first folded edge.

Button side

2. To make the button-hole side of the flip side, sew blue 4½" x 9¼" rectangles to the top and bottom of the white 6½" x 9¼" rectangle. Press the seam allowances toward the blue rectangles. Add the blue 4½" x 14½" rectangle to the left side of this unit. Press the seam allowances toward the blue rectangle. Join the white 1¾" x 13¼" strips to the top and bottom of this unit, and then

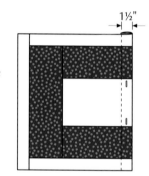

Buttonhole side

add the remaining 1¾" x 17" strip to the left side; press the seam allowances toward the blue rectangles after each white strip is added. Fuse the remaining interfacing strip to the wrong side of the right edge and fold it under 1½" twice. Make vertical buttonholes 2" from each side of the band center.

3. Layer the buttonhole band over the button band and stay stitch across the band ends.

4. Place the white 17" square and flip-side pieces wrong sides together. Stitch the edges together using a scant ½" seam allowance. Bind the edges using the white 3⅛"-wide strips and a ½" seam allowance. Refer to "Binding" (page 7) as needed.

5. Mark the button locations on the button band to correspond to the buttonholes and sew the buttons to the band. Insert the pillow form into the cover.

Make Your Bed
ELEGANT

Rich silk fabric, covered buttons, and tassels—they make everything special,
so don't be afraid to step out of the cotton comfort zone and pamper yourself.
Although it needs to be treated with a little extra care, silk is well worth the effort.
(See "Working with Silk" on page 64 for a few tips to put you at ease.)

Floral Silk Runner

Finished Runner: 29¾" x 110¾" • Finished Block: 14" x 14"

MATERIALS

Yardage is based on 54"-wide fabric unless otherwise noted.

1⅜ yards of red floral silk for front

1 yard of cream floral silk for front

1¼ yards of gold solid silk for side setting triangles, end borders, and binding

3⅝ yards of 42"-wide cotton fabric for backing

34" x 116" piece of batting

Two 6"-long tassels

4 covered-button forms, 1½" in diameter

2 covered-button forms, 1¼" in diameter

CUTTING

From the red floral, cut:
   8 squares, 15" x 15"

From the cream floral, cut:
   5 squares, 15" x 15"

From the gold solid, cut:
   1 strip, 7" x 54"

From the *lengthwise grain* of the remaining gold solid, cut:
   4 strips, 4½" x 30"

From the *bias* of the remaining gold solid, cut:
   Enough 2½"-wide strips to yield a 270" length after piecing

PIECING THE ROWS

Sew all seams using ½" seam allowances unless otherwise noted.

1. Crosscut the gold 7" x 54" strip at a 45° angle to make six triangles with a 14"-wide base.

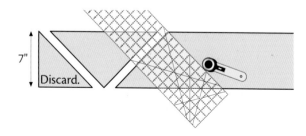

Working with Silk

Silk is a rich fabric, so it needs to be treated with a little more care than a cotton fabric. Because the edges tend to ravel, use ½"- rather than ¼"-wide seam allowances. Silk may have natural slubs or a sheen that can make the color appear different when viewed from different angles. To eliminate color shifts in your finished project, make sure to run all of the pieces the same way. A pin marking the front and top of each piece is an easy way to keep track of which way is up.

2. Referring to the assembly diagram (page 65) so that the fabric nap is running the same way on each piece when the rows are assembled, sew the red squares, cream squares, and gold triangles into rows as shown. Note that two of the rows will be flipped when the table runner is assembled. Press the seam allowances toward the red squares.

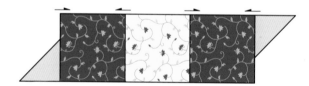

Make 1.

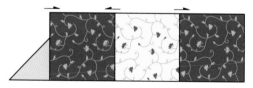

Make 2.

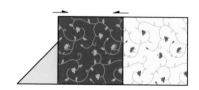

Make 2.

ASSEMBLING THE RUNNER

1. Stack the gold 4½" x 30" strips, two with right sides down and two with right sides up, and trim one end at a 45° angle to make the end borders.

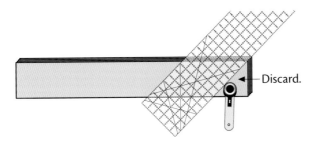

2. Refer to the assembly diagram below to arrange the pieced rows and the end borders as shown. Sew the rows together, and then attach the end borders, referring to "Borders with Mitered Corners" (page 6) as needed.

Runner assembly

3. Trim the long sides of the runner 5" away from the points of the cream squares.

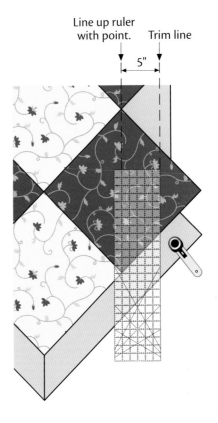

FINISHING

1. Refer to "Making the Quilt Sandwich" (page 7) to layer the bed-runner top, batting, and backing. Be careful to square up the on-point squares with a ruler or laser level because they tend to stretch out of shape.

2. Quilt as desired. For quilting this runner, less is more! Quilt by stitching in the ditch around the red and cream squares with red thread and between the gold triangles and cream squares with gold thread to make the quilting disappear. After quilting, trim the batting and backing even with the runner top.

3. Bind the edges using the gold 2½"-wide bias strips and a ⅜" seam allowance. Refer to "Binding" (page 7) as needed.

4. Refer to the package instructions to cover the button forms with leftover cream floral fabric. Sew the 1½"-diameter covered buttons at each point where the red squares meet in the center of the runner. Sew the 1¼"-diameter covered buttons at each end point and attach the tassels to the buttons (see the photo on page 4).

Floral Silk Shams

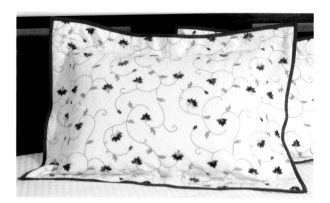

Finished Shams: 26" x 36"

MATERIALS
(for two queen-size shams)

Yardage is based on 54"-wide fabric unless otherwise noted.

1⅔ yards of cream floral silk for front

1⅔ yards of cream solid silk for flip side

1 yard of red solid silk for bias binding

4 yards of 42"-wide plain cotton or muslin for lining

54" x 77" piece of batting

⅞ yard of 20"-wide lightweight fusible interfacing

6 covered button forms, 1¼" in diameter

CUTTING

From the cream floral, cut:
 2 rectangles, 27" x 37"

From the cream solid, cut:
 2 rectangles, 27" x 26½"
 2 rectangles, 27" x 19"

From the interfacing, cut:
 4 strips, 1½" x 27"

From the batting, cut:
 2 rectangles, 27" x 37"
 2 rectangles, 27" x 23½"
 2 rectangles, 27" x 16"

From the backing fabric, cut:
 2 rectangles, 27" x 37"
 2 rectangles, 27" x 23½"
 2 rectangles, 27" x 16"

From the red solid, cut:
 Enough 3⅛"-wide bias strips to make a 280"-long
  strip after piecing

MAKING THE SHAMS

Refer to "Making the Sham" (page 15) to make two shams, following "The Still Easy but Reversible Sham" instructions. Back the front and flip-side pieces with batting and lining fabric and cover the button forms with leftover cream solid fabric before sewing them to the button band. Bind the edges using the red solid 3⅛"-wide strips and a ½" seam allowance.

Floral Silk Pillow

Finished Pillow: 12" x 18"

MATERIALS

Yardage is based on 54"-wide fabric.

½ yard of red floral silk for front and flip side

¼ yard of gold solid silk for center-square binding

7" x 7" square of cream floral silk for center square

7" x 7" piece of batting

⅛ yard of 20"-wide lightweight fusible interfacing

1 yard of 1¾"-wide gold fringe

2 same-sized buttons, ⅝" to 1¼" in diameter

⅛ yard of 20"-wide lightweight fusible interfacing

12" x 18" pillow form

CUTTING

From the red floral, cut:

1 rectangle, 13" x 19"

1 rectangle, 13" x 15½"

1 rectangle, 13" x 12"

From the *bias* of the gold solid, cut:

Enough 3"-wide strips to yield a 34"-long strip
after piecing

From the interfacing, cut:

2 strips, 1½" x 13"

MAKING THE PILLOW TOP

1. Layer the cream floral 7" square over the batting square and baste around the edges.

2. Refer to "Binding" (page 7) to position a single layer of the gold bias strip on the square (do not fold the strip in half lengthwise), right sides together, and bind the edges using a ¾" seam allowance. Turn the binding to the batting side of the square and baste it in place with a loose running stitch, mitering the corners and making sure the stitches don't go through to the front.

3. Center the bound square diagonally on the red floral 13" x 19" rectangle and stitch in the ditch around the inside of the binding. Cut two 12" lengths of fringe. With the fringe pointed toward the pillow center, center and stitch a length to each end of the rectangle, leaving ½" of the rectangle fabric exposed along the sides.

4. Using the remaining red rectangles, make the un-backed pillow flip side, following the instructions for "Making the Flip Side" (page 14) for un-backed pieces. Also make the following adjustments: interface the 13"-long edge and make a buttonhole at the center of the buttonhole band and 4" from each side of the center.

5. Align the edge of the larger flip-side piece with the end of the front piece, *right sides together*; baste. Align the button band of the smaller flip-side piece with the buttonhole band on the larger piece, overlapping the bands 1½"; baste across the band ends. If needed, trim any extra fabric on the end flush with the front. Stitch around the edges using a ½" seam allowance and being careful not to catch the loose edges of the fringe in the seam.

6. Clip the corners and turn the pillow to the right side. Sew the buttons to the button band to correspond to the buttonhole locations.

7. Insert the pillow form into the pillow cover.

Make Your Bed
NATURAL

This runner design is subtle with a little graphic pop. While the flip side of each piece shown is a simple green fabric, it would be easy to duplicate the front design in pretty pastels and substitute the leaf appliqués with fun flowers for a peek into springtime. Coordinating the fabrics on each side of the runner with the shams and fringed bands gives many different options with a few simple pieces.

Forest Runner

Finished Runner: 30" x 99", including 7" detachable fringed bands

MATERIALS

Yardage is based on 42"-wide fabric unless otherwise noted.

3½ yards of soft green fabric for flip side

6 fat quarters *each* of assorted gold, light green, and dark green fabrics for background

1⅛ yards of dark gold fabric for fringed bands front and binding

½ yard of medium brown fabric for tree appliqués

⅓ yard of dark brown fabric for tree appliqués

6" x 8" rectangle *each* of yellow, orange, and red fabrics for leaf appliqués

35" x 93" piece of batting

⅓ yard of paper-backed fusible web

1 yard of 20"-wide lightweight fusible interfacing

2 yards of gold 1¼"-wide fringe

12 buttons, ¾" in diameter

CUTTING

Before any fabric is cut, you need to decide which fabric goes where. Referring to the assembly diagram (page 71), lay out your fabrics in columns, labeling each color 1 through 6 for each of the six columns on the quilt. For example, the light green fabric that goes in column 3 would be labeled LG 3. Note: Gold, light green, and dark green fabrics labeled 2, 4, and 6 will not need to be cut at this time.

From *each* of the gold 1 and 3, light green 1 and 3, and dark green 1 and 3 fabrics, cut:

1 rectangle, 11" x 18" (6 total)

From *each* of the gold 5, light green 5, and dark green 5 fabrics, cut:

1 rectangle, 15" x 18" (3 total)

From the dark brown fabric, cut:

3 strips, 2½" x 36"

From the medium brown fabric, cut:

3 strips, 4½" x 36"

From the paper-backed fusible web, cut:

3 rectangles, 6" x 8"

From the dark gold fabric, cut:

2 strips, 8½" x 31"

7 strips, 2½" x 42"

From the soft green fabric, cut:

2 strips, 8½" x 31"

From the interfacing, cut:

2 strips, 2" x 31"

MAKING THE COLUMNS

1. On a cutting mat, lay the gold 1 and dark green 1 rectangles right side up, aligning the vertical edges and butting up the horizontal edges as shown.

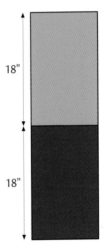

2. Roughly center the light green 1 rectangle over the gold and dark green rectangles right side up, aligning the vertical edges.

3. Make two random diagonal cuts across the width of the layered rectangles. The diagonals need to be cut in opposite directions to make a shape that is narrower on one side than the other. Discard the pieces indicated below and then sew the remaining pieces back together.

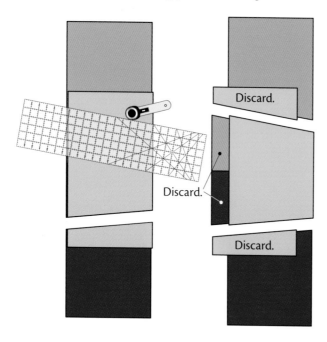

4. Repeat steps 1–3 for the remaining columns, using the uncut fat quarters for columns 2, 4, and 6. Work from left to right, and lay the previous column to the left of the one being cut to help space the seam lines so they don't line up.

5. Trim the width of each column as follows:

Column	Trimmed Width
1 and 3	10½"
2, 4, and 6	18½"
5	14½"

6. Trim the length of each column to 30½".

APPLIQUÉING AND ASSEMBLING THE RUNNER

1. To make the tree appliqués, sew each dark brown strip to a medium brown strip along the long edges. Press the seam allowances to one side. Trim both of the long edges of each strip at an angle, beginning slightly in from the bottom of the strips and angling the ruler up to 1" in from the edge at the top of the strips. The width of the strips after cutting should measure 4" to 5" at the top and 5" to 6" at the bottom. Press the long edges under ¼" and appliqué a tree to columns 2, 4, and 6. Trim the top and bottom of the appliqués even with the columns.

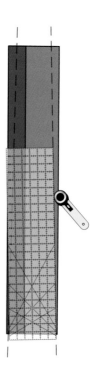

2. To make the leaf appliqués, trace the leaf pattern (page 75) onto the paper side of each fusible-web rectangle. Follow the manufacturer's instructions to apply a fusible-web rectangle to the wrong side of each leaf fabric. Cut out each leaf. Remove the paper backing and fuse the leaves to columns 2, 4, and 5, referring to the assembly diagram for placement. Stitch around each leaf using a satin stitch or the stitch of your choice.

3. Machine satin stitch each leaf's stem, widening the stitch as you stitch down the stem. Straight stitch the veins of each leaf, referring to the pattern for placement.

4. Sew the columns together in order along their long edges.

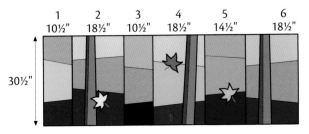

Runner assembly

MAKING THE FRINGED BANDS

1. Fold the dark gold and soft green 8½" x 31" strips in half crosswise. Stack the folded rectangles on top of each other, aligning the edges. To cut the angle, place your ruler at the tip of the folded end and 4" in from the long sides at the opposite end; cut. Discard the triangular pieces. Unfold the bands.

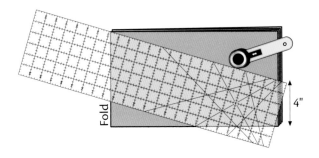

2. Cut the fringe in half. On the right side of each dark gold band, stitch the lip edge of the fringe to the angled edge of the band as shown, leaving ½" of band fabric exposed at each end; trim away any excess fringe.

3. Fuse a strip of interfacing to the wrong side of each dark gold band along the straight edge. Layer each interfaced band with a soft green band, right sides together, with the fringe tucked inside the band. Stitch along all of the edges using a ½" seam allowance and leaving an opening along the straight edge for turning.

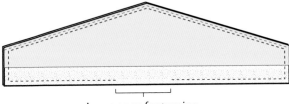

Leave open for turning.

4. Clip the corners at an angle, being careful not to cut into the fringe. Turn the bands to the right side and hand stitch the openings closed. Make six buttonholes ¾" from the straight edge of each band, spacing a buttonhole ¾" from each end and the remaining buttonholes 5½" apart.

71

FINISHING

1. Refer to "Making the Quilt Sandwich" (page 7) to layer the bed-runner top, batting, and soft green flip side; baste the layers together.
2. Quilt as desired. I quilted the runner with an allover fern-leaf design. After quilting, trim the batting and backing even with the top.
3. Bind the edges using the dark gold 2½"-wide strips and a ⅜" seam allowance. Refer to "Binding" (page 7) as needed.
4. On the runner flip side, sew the buttons to the runner ends to correspond to the fringed-band buttonholes.

Forest Pillow

Finished Pillow: 20" x 20"

MATERIALS

Yardage is based on 42"-wide fabric.

⅔ yard of fabric for back

½ yard of dark gold fabric for border

1 fat quarter of dark green fabric for background

1 fat eighth *each* of gold and light green fabrics for background

6" x 8" rectangle of orange fabric for leaf appliqué

⅝ yard of plain cotton or muslin for front lining

6" x 8" piece of paper-backed fusible web

⅛ yard of 20"-wide lightweight fusible interfacing

3 same-sized buttons, ⅝" to 1¼" in diameter

4 tassels, 3¾" long

20" x 20" square pillow form

CUTTING

From *each* of the gold and light green fabrics, cut:
1 rectangle, 7" x 15" (2 total)

From the dark green fabric, cut:
1 rectangle, 11" x 15"

From the dark gold fabric, cut:
1 rectangle, 9" x 21"
2 rectangles, 3¾" x 17¼"
1 rectangle, 3¾" x 21"

From the interfacing, cut:
2 strips, 1½" x 21"

From the lining fabric, cut:
1 square, 22" x 22"

From the back fabric, cut:
1 square, 21" x 21"

MAKING THE PILLOW

1. To make the center square, refer to steps 1–3 of "Making the Columns" (page 69) to lay out and cut the gold, light green, and dark green rectangles; sew the pieces together. Trim the piece to 14½" x 17¼". **Note:** The bottom 3" of the dark green fabric will be turned under to make the buttonhole band.
2. Refer to step 2 of "Appliquéing and Assembling the Runner" (page 70) to make the leaf appliqué and stitch it to the center square.
3. Sew the dark gold 3¾" x 17¼" border strips to the sides of the center square. Press the seam allowances toward the border strips. Sew the 3¾" x 21" border strip to the top of the center square. Press the seam allowances toward the border strip.
4. To make the buttonhole band, fuse an interfacing strip to the wrong side of the green bottom edge of the center quare and fold it under 1½" twice. Unfold the band once and lay the lining fabric on the wrong side so one long edge butts up to the fold. Refold the band over

the lining and baste around the raw edges. Trim the lining even with the front. Make a vertical buttonhole at the band center and 6" from each side of the center.

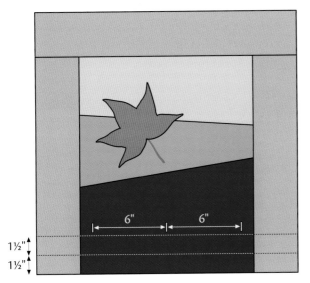

Buttonhole side

5. To make the button band, fuse an interfacing strip to the wrong side of one long edge of the dark gold 9" x 21" rectangle and fold it under 1½" twice; stitch close to the first folded edge.

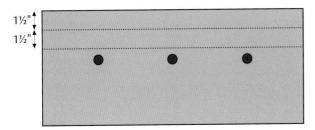

Button side

6. With right sides up, layer the buttonhole band over the button band and baste across the band ends.

7. Place a tassel at each corner of the pillow top, right side up, with the fringed ends pointing toward the center of the pillow and the cord at the top of the tassels in the seam allowance. Stay stitch across the cords.

8. Layer the pillow top and pillow back right sides together. Stitch the edges together using a ½" seam allowance. Be careful not to catch the

tassels in the seam. Trim the corners without trimming the tassel cords and turn the pillow to the right side. Sew the buttons to the button band to correspond to the buttonholes. Insert the pillow form into the cover.

Fringed Pillow

Finished Pillow: 12" x 18"

MATERIALS (for one pillow)

Yardage is based on 42"-wide fabric.

½ yard *total* of assorted green fabrics for front

½ yard of coordinating fabric for flip side

⅛ yard of 20"-wide lightweight fusible interfacing

2 yards of 1¼"-wide fringe

2 same-sized buttons, ¾" to 1" in diameter

12" x 18" pillow form

CUTTING

From the coordinating flip-side fabric, cut:
　　1 rectangle, 13" x 15½"
　　1 rectangle, 13" x 11"

From the interfacing, cut:
　　2 strips, 1½" x 13"

MAKING THE PILLOW

1. To make the pillow front, cut the assorted green fabrics into strips between 2½" and 6½" wide and 14" long. Vary the strip width from top to bottom if desired. Piece the strips together along the long edges to make a rectangle at least 14" x 19". Trim the piece to 13" x 18".

2. Refer to "The Still Easy but Reversible Pillows" (page 13) to complete the pillow, making the following adjustments: fuse the interfacing strips to the 13" edges of the coordinating fabric rectangles, make a buttonhole 2" from each side of the center on the interfaced buttonhole band, and sew the fringe to the front piece. Insert the pillow form into the cover.

Forest Shams

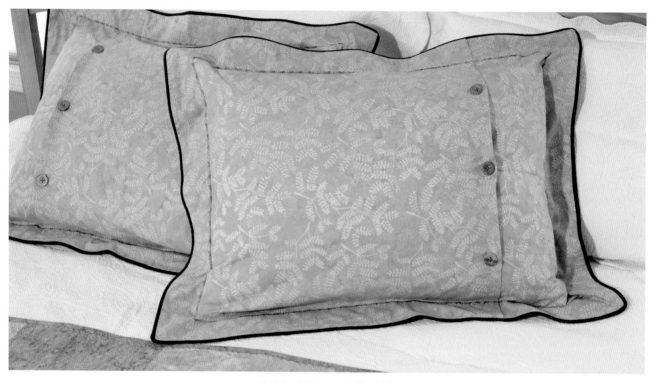

Finished Shams: 26" x 32"

The shams are made of rich batik fabrics in gold on the front and soft green on the flip side, both of which match the runner. You can decide each morning which beautiful batik to show off! Refer to "Shams: The Same but Different!" (page 15) for instructions.

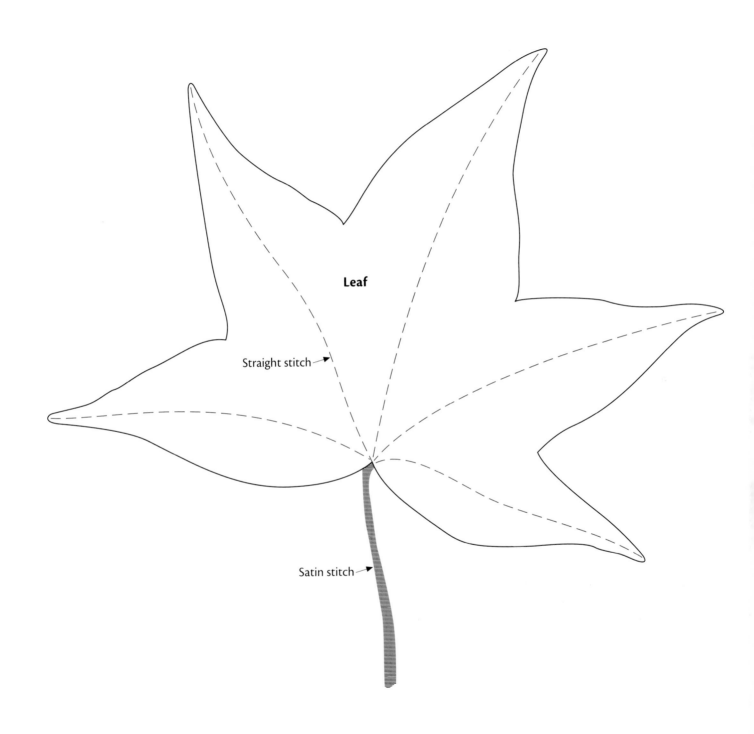

Leaf

Straight stitch →

Satin stitch →

Make Your Bed
CHEERFUL

Color is the secret to this runner's success! Gradations of red, blue, green, and purple set the stars in motion. Using a reversible binding allows the flip side to be any fabric you wish.

76

Friendship Star Runner

Finished Runner: 22½" x 104½"

MATERIALS

Yardage is based on 42"-wide fabric and includes enough to make extra units for "Friendship Star Pillow" (page 81). You will need five gradations of fabrics ranging from lightest (1) to darkest (5) in red, blue, green, and purple.

3½ yards of medium fabric for flip side and flip-side reversible binding

1⅜ yards of black fabric for blocks, border, and reversible binding

¼ yard *each* of green fabrics 1, 2, 3, and 4

¼ yard *each* of purple fabrics 1, 2, 3, and 4

¼ yard *each* of red fabrics 3, 4, and 5

¼ yard *each* of blue fabrics 3, 4, and 5

⅛ yard *each* of red fabrics 1 and 2

⅛ yard *each* of blue fabrics 1 and 2

⅛ yard *each* of green fabric 5 and purple fabric 5

⅔ yard of cream fabric for stars

28" x 110" piece of batting

CUTTING

From the black fabric, cut:
  10 strips, 2½" x 42"; crosscut *4 of the strips* into:
    37 squares, 2½" x 2½"
    2 strips, 2½" x 12"
  9 strips, 1½" x 42"; crosscut into:
    8 strips, 1½" x 28"
    4 strips, 1½" x 12"
    14 rectangles, 1½" x 2½"
  7 strips, 1" x 42" (cut strips 2½" wide if not making reversible binding)

From *each* of the red 3 and blue 3 fabrics, cut:
  1 strip, 3½" x 42"; crosscut into:
    1 strip, 3½" x 28" (2 total)
    1 strip, 3½" x 12" (2 total)

From *each* of the green 3 and purple 3 fabrics, cut:
  1 strip, 3½" x 28" (2 total)
  1 strip, 1½" x 42" (2 total)

From *each* of the red 1 and blue 1 fabrics, cut:
  1 strip, 1½" x 28" (2 total)

From *each* of the green 5 and purple 5 fabrics, cut:
  1 strip, 1½" x 42"; crosscut into:
    1 strip, 1½" x 28" (2 total)
    1 strip, 1½" x 12" (2 total)

From *each* of the red 2 and blue 2 fabrics, cut:
  1 strip, 2½" x 42"; crosscut into:
    1 strip, 2½" x 28" (2 total)
    1 strip, 2½" x 12" (2 total)

From *each* of the green 4 and purple 4 fabrics, cut:
  1 strip, 2½" x 28" (2 total)
  1 strip, 1½" x 42" (2 total)

From *each* of the red 4 and 5 fabrics and the blue 4 and 5 fabrics, cut:
  3 strips, 1½" x 42" (12 total)

From *each* of the green 1 and 2 fabrics and the purple 1 and 2 fabrics, cut:
  3 strips, 1½" x 42" (12 total)

From the cream fabric, cut:
  8 strips, 2½" x 42"; crosscut into 114 squares, 2½" x 2½"

From the flip-side binding fabric, cut:
  7 strips, 2" x 42"

MAKING THE UNITS

1. To make the A units, sew a 1½" x 28" black strip to each of the 3½" x 28" red 3, blue 3, green 3, and purple 3 strips along the long edges to make strip sets. Press the seam allowances toward the black strips. Crosscut each strip set into 18 segments, 1½" wide.

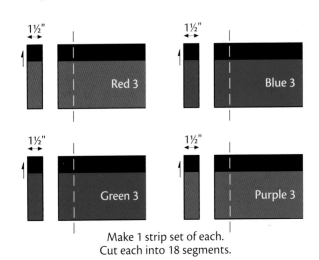

Make 1 strip set of each.
Cut each into 18 segments.

2. Sew a 1½" x 28" black strip to each of the 1½" x 28" red 1, blue 1, green 5, and purple 5 strips along the long edges as shown. Add the 2½" x 28" blue 2, red 2, purple 4, and green 4 strips to make strip sets as shown. Press the seam allowances toward the black strips. Crosscut each strip set into 18 segments, 1½" wide.

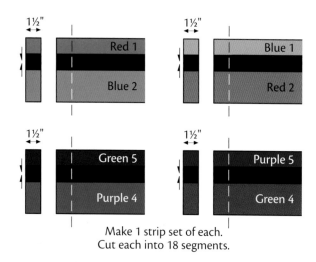

Make 1 strip set of each.
Cut each into 18 segments.

3. Sew the segments from steps 1 and 2 together as shown to make 18 of each color combination.

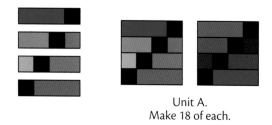

Unit A.
Make 18 of each.

4. To make the B and C units, sew each 1½" x 42" blue 4 strip to a 1½" x 42" blue 5 strip to make a strip set. Repeat with the 1½" x 42" red 4 and red 5 strips, the 1½" x 42" green 1 and 2 strips, and the 1½" x 42" purple 1 and 2 strips. Press the seam allowances toward the darker strips.

Crosscut each strip set into the number of segments shown.

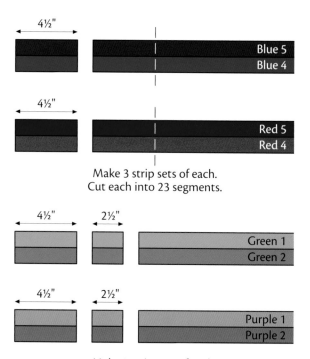

Make 3 strip sets of each.
Cut each into 23 segments.

Make 3 strip sets of each.
Cut each into 16 segments, 4½" wide,
and 7 segments, 2½" wide.

5. Mark a diagonal line from corner to corner on the wrong side of 92 cream squares. Layer a cream square over the left end of each segment from step 4 as shown, right sides together. Be careful that the strip-set segment is oriented with the correct fabric on top. It's easy to get these units upside down. I know from experience! Stitch a thread's width to the outside of each marked line (toward the strip-segment corner). Trim ¼" from the stitching lines. Press the seam allowances toward the strip segment.

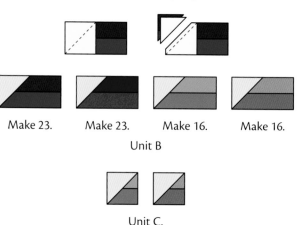

Make 23.   Make 23.   Make 16.   Make 16.

Unit B

Unit C.
Make 7 of each.

6. To make the D units, sew a 1½" x 12" black strip to each of the 3½" x 12" red 3 and blue 3 strips along the long edges to make a strip set. Crosscut the strip sets into seven segments, 1½" wide.

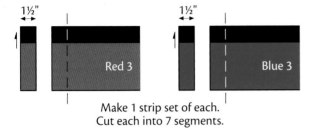

Make 1 strip set of each.
Cut each into 7 segments.

7. Sew a 2½" x 12" black strip to each of the 2½" x 12" red 2 and blue 2 strips along the long edges to make a strip set. Crosscut the strip sets into seven segments, 1½" wide.

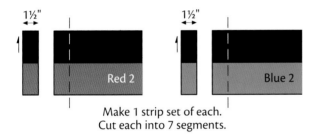

Make 1 strip set of each.
Cut each into 7 segments.

8. Sew the segments from steps 6 and 7 together as shown to make seven red units and seven blue units.

Unit D.
Make 7 of each.

9. To make the E units, sew the 1½" x 42" green 3 and 4 strips together along the long edges to make a strip set. Repeat with the 1½" x 42" purple 3 and 4 strips. Press the seam allowances toward the darker strips. Crosscut each strip set into seven segments, 2½" wide.

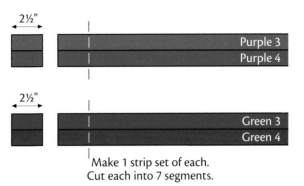

Make 1 strip set of each.
Cut each into 7 segments.

10. Sew a 1½" x 12" black strip to the 1½" x 12" purple 5 and green 5 strips. Press the seam allowances toward the black strips. Crosscut each strip set into seven segments, 1½" wide.

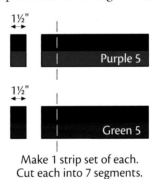

Make 1 strip set of each.
Cut each into 7 segments.

11. Sew the 1½" x 2½" black rectangles and the units from steps 9 and 10 together as shown to make seven purple units and seven green units.

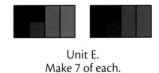

Unit E.
Make 7 of each.

ASSEMBLING THE RUNNER

1. Set aside two red-and-blue A units, two green-and-purple A units, and one each of the blue, red, green, and purple B units for the "Friendship Star Pillow" (page 81). Refer to the assembly diagram at right to lay out the remaining units and the cream and black 2½" squares into horizontal rows as shown. Sew the pieces in each row together. Press the seam allowances in opposite directions from row to row. Sew the rows together.

2. Sew three of the remaining 2½" x 42" black strips together end to end. Repeat to make a total of two strips. Measure the long straight edges of the runner. Trim each of the pieced strips to the length measured. Pin, and then sew the strips to the long, straight edges of the runner. Set aside the remainder of the strips for the end borders.

3. Trim the ends of the runner at a 45° angle by placing the ¼" line of your ruler through the center of the unit A black squares. Cut all the way from the 2½" black square at the end of the runner through the side borders.

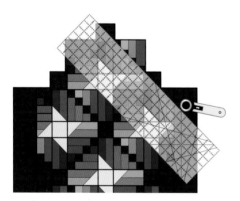

Cut ¼" from the square centers.

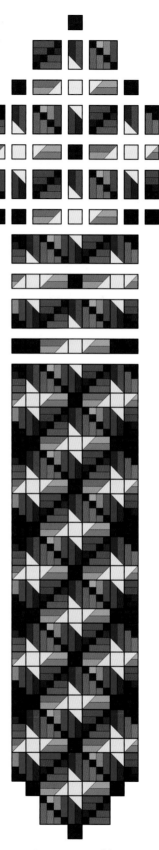

Runner assembly

4. Sew the leftover border strips to the angled ends of the runner, aligning the strip at the points and extending them past the sides. Trim the excess even with the sides.

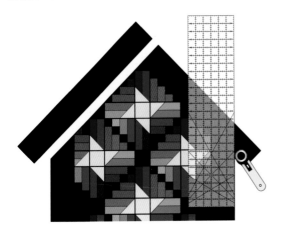

FINISHING

1. Refer to "Making the Quilt Sandwich" (page 7) to layer the bed-runner top, batting, and backing fabric. Baste the layers together.
2. Quilt as desired. I used black metallic thread on top and blue variegated thread in the bobbin and quilted an allover swirl pattern. After quilting, trim the batting and backing even with the runner top.
3. Refer to "Making a Reversible Binding" (page 84) to bind the edges with a reversible binding strip using the 1"-wide black binding strips for the front and the 2"-wide medium blue binding strips for the flip side.

Friendship Star Pillow

Finished Pillow: 19" x 19"

MATERIALS

Yardage is based on 42"-wide fabric.

2 *each* of red-and-blue and green-and-purple A units set aside from "Friendship Star Runner" (page 77)

1 *each* of red, blue, green, and purple B units set aside from "Friendship Star Runner"

⅝ yard of black fabric for borders and reversible binding

¾ yard of medium blue fabric for flip side and flip-side reversible binding

2½" x 2½" square of cream fabric

Scraps of red, blue, green, and purple fabrics for pieced border

20" x 20" piece of plain cotton or muslin for lining

20" x 20" piece of batting

⅛ yard of 20"-wide lightweight fusible interfacing

3 same-sized buttons, ⅝" to 1¼" in diameter

18" x 18" square pillow form

CUTTING

From the red scraps, cut:
    4 rectangles, 1½" x 2½"
    4 squares, 1½" x 1½"

From *each* of the blue, green, and purple scraps, cut:
    8 rectangles, 1½" x 2½"

From the black fabric, cut:
2 strips, 2½" x 10½"
2 strips, 2½" x 14½"
2 strips, 1¾" x 16½"
2 strips, 1¾" x 19"
2 strips, 1" x 42"

From the medium blue fabric, cut:
2 strips, 2" x 42"

MAKING THE PILLOW

1. Arrange the A and B units and the cream 2½" square into three vertical rows as shown. Sew the units in each row together. Press the seam allowances toward the A units. Sew the rows together. Press the seam allowances toward the center row.

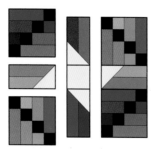 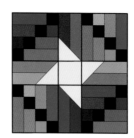

Make 1.

2. Refer to the pillow assembly diagram at right to sew the black 2½" x 10½" strips to the top and bottom of the block. Press the seam allowances toward the strips. Sew the black 2½" x 14½" strips to the sides of the block. Press the seam allowances toward the strips.

3. Sew two purple, two green, two blue, and one red rectangle together as shown. Repeat to make a total of four pieced border strips. Sew pieced border strips to the top and bottom of the pillow top. Press the seam allowances toward the black borders. Add a red square to the ends of the two remaining border strips. Sew these border strips to the sides of the pillow top. Press the seam allowances toward the black borders.

Make 4.

4. Sew the black 1¾" x 16½" border strips to the top and bottom of the pillow top. Press the seam allowances toward the newly added strips. Sew the black 1¾" x 19" strips to the sides of the pillow top. Press the seam allowance toward the newly added strips.

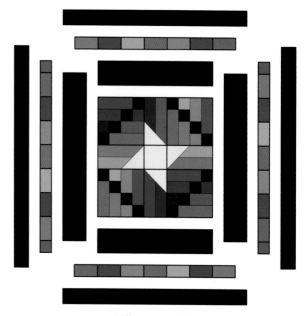

Pillow assembly

FINISHING

1. Refer to "Making the Quilt Sandwich" (page 7) to layer the front backing piece, batting, and pieced top; baste the layers together. Quilt as desired. I used the same allover swirl pattern that I used for the runner. After quilting, trim the lining and batting even with the pillow top.

2. Refer to "Making the Flip Side" (page 14) to make the pillow flip-side and "Assembling the Pillow" (page 14) to sew the top and flip-side pieces together. Refer to "Making a Reversible Binding" (page 84) to bind the edges with a reversible binding strip made from the black 1"-wide strips and the medium blue flip-side 2"-wide strips. Sew the buttons to the flip-side button band to correspond to the buttonholes. Insert the pillow form into the cover.

Gradation Pillow

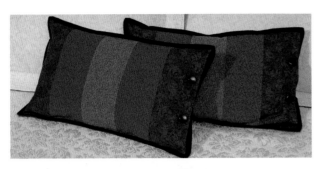

Finished Pillow: 12½" x 20½"

MATERIALS (for one pillow)

Yardage is based on 42"-wide fabric unless otherwise noted.

1 fat eighth *each* of yellow, gold, orange, dark orange, and red fabrics for front

1 fat quarter *each* of medium blue and dark blue fabrics for flip side

1 fat eighth of light blue for flip side

¼ yard of blue fabric for reversible binding

⅛ yard of black fabric for reversible binding

⅛ yard of 20"-wide lightweight fusible interfacing

2 same-sized buttons, ⅝" to 1¼" in diameter

12" x 20" pillow form

CUTTING

From the yellow, gold, orange, dark orange, red, and light blue fabrics, cut:

1 rectangle, 4½" x 13" (6 total)

From the medium blue fabric, cut:

2 rectangles, 4½" x 13"

From the dark blue fabric, cut:

2 rectangles, 4½" x 13"

1 rectangle, 7½" x 13"

From the interfacing, cut:

2 strips, 1½" x 13"

From the blue fabric for binding, cut:

2 strips, 2" x 42"

From the black fabric for binding, cut:

2 strips, 1" x 42"

MAKING THE PILLOW

1. To make the front, sew the 4½" x 13" rectangles together in the following order: yellow, gold, orange, dark orange, and red. Press the seam allowances toward the red rectangle.

2. To make the flip side, sew the 4½" x 13" rectangles together in the following order: dark blue, medium blue, light blue, medium blue. Sew the dark blue 7½" x 13" rectangle to the long raw edge of the medium blue rectangle on the right-hand side of the unit. Press the seam allowances toward the dark blue rectangles.

3. To make the buttonhole band, fuse a strip of interfacing to the wrong side of the dark blue 7½" x 13" rectangle along the long edge. Fold under the interfaced edge 1½" twice. Make two vertical buttonholes in the band, 2" on each side of the center and ¾" from the edge.

4. To make the button band, fold the remaining dark blue 4½" x 13" rectangle in half lengthwise, wrong sides together; press. Open up the piece to the wrong side and fuse the remaining strip of interfacing next to the fold line. Refold the strip.

5. With the 13" edges aligned, place the button band on the wrong side of the red rectangle of the front piece. Stitch along the rectangle long edge using a scant ½" seam allowance. Layer the flip side over the front, wrong sides together, with the buttonhole band overlapping the button band. Sew around the edges using a

scant ½" seam allowance. Refer to "Making a Reversible Binding" below to bind the edges with a reversible binding strip made from the blue 2"-wide strips and the black 1"-wide strips. Sew the buttons to the button band to correspond to the buttonholes. Insert the pillow form into the cover.

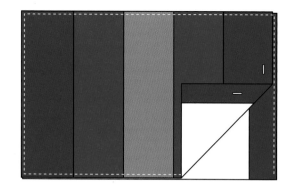

Friendship Star Shams

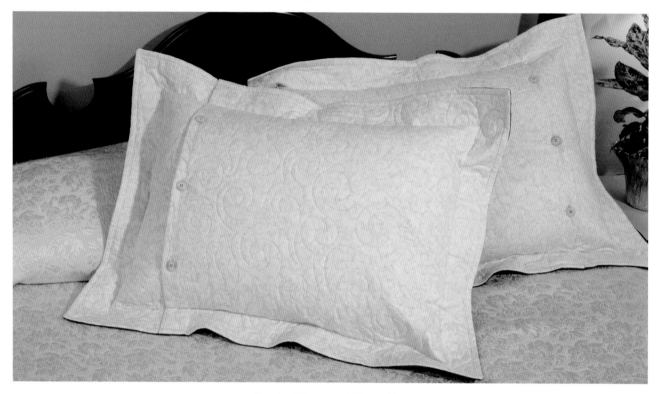

Finished Sham: 26½" x 34½"

The Shams are made of rich cream fabric on the front and medium blue fabric on the flip side. Refer to "Shams: The Same but Different!" (page 15) for instructions.

MAKING A REVERSIBLE BINDING

Sometimes, the same fabric on both sides of the binding just won't do. These instructions make a ⅜" binding with different fabrics on each side. Cut strips crosswise for double binding—not on the bias.

1. Cut the binding fabric for the front of the quilt 1" wide. Cut the binding fabric for the back of the quilt 2" wide.

2. Sew the ends of the 1"-wide strips together at a 45° angle and press the seam allowances open. Repeat for the 2"-wide strips.

3. Sew the 1"-wide strip to the 2"-wide strip along the long edges using a ¼" seam allowance. Press the seam allowances toward the front fabric. Fold the strip in half lengthwise, wrong sides together; press.

4. Trim one end at a 45° angle and press ¼" to the wrong side.

5. Attach the binding following steps 3–9 of "Attaching Binding" (page 7).

Make Your Bed
EARTHY

Despite the traditional Maple Leaf and Rail Fence blocks used for this grouping,
this is not your grandmother's quilt! Thread-painted trees are created on soft, supple
suede, which is also incorporated into the background, adding a bit of surprise and texture.
Color-drenched batiks grace the flip side.

Leaves-and-Trees Runner

Finished Runner: 24½" x 108½"

MATERIALS

Yardage is based on 42"-wide fabric unless otherwise noted.

6 fat quarters of assorted cream prints for background

1 yard of yellow faux suede for Tree blocks

¾ yard of green faux suede for Tree blocks

⅔ yard of cream faux suede for background

⅝ yard of green fabric for large leaves

⅝ yard of red fabric for small leaves

½ yard of tan faux suede for Tree blocks

⅝ yard of tan fabric for binding

3¼ yards of fabric for backing fabric (only needed if not using the pieced flip side)

30" x 114" piece of batting

2½ yards of 20"-wide fusible tear-away stabilizer

Variegated brown rayon thread

CUTTING

From the cream faux suede, cut:
  3 squares, 4⅞" x 4⅞"
  18 squares, 4½" x 4½"
  11 squares, 2⅞" x 2⅞"
  18 squares, 2½" x 2½"
  1 rectangle, 2½" x 4½"

From *each* of the 6 assorted cream prints, cut:
  2 strips, 4½" x 20"; crosscut into:
      7 squares, 4½" x 4½" (42 total; you'll use 38)
      2 rectangles, 2½" x 4½" (12 total; you'll use 8) 1 strip, 5" x 20" (6 total). From the strip, cut 1 square, 4⅞" x 4⅞" (6 total; you'll use 3).
  Cut the remainder of the strip in half lengthwise and crosscut into 11 squares, 2½" x 2½" (66 total; you'll use 62).
  1 strip, 2⅞" x 20"; crosscut into 4 squares, 2⅞" x 2⅞" (24 total; you'll use 21)

From the green fabric, cut:
  6 squares, 4⅞" x 4⅞"
  8 squares, 4½" x 4½"
  14 squares, 2⅞" x 2⅞"
  17 squares, 2½" x 2½"
  3 rectangles, 2" x 7"

From the red fabric, cut:
  28 squares, 2⅞" x 2⅞"
  52 squares, 2½" x 2½"
  16 strips, 1" x 4"

From the yellow faux suede, cut:
  3 squares, 14" x 14"

From the green faux suede, cut:
  3 rectangles, 11" x 14"

From the tan faux suede, cut:
  3 rectangles, 8" x 14"

From the stabilizer, cut:
  3 squares, 14" x 14"
  3 rectangles, 11" x 14"
  3 rectangles, 8" x 14"

From the tan fabric for binding, cut:
  8 strips, 2¼" x 42"

MAKING THE BACKGROUND UNITS

1. Refer to "Making Half-Square-Triangle Units" (page 5) to make large half-square-triangle units using 4⅞" squares. Layer each of three green squares with a cream faux suede square to make six units. Repeat with three green and three assorted cream print squares to make six units.

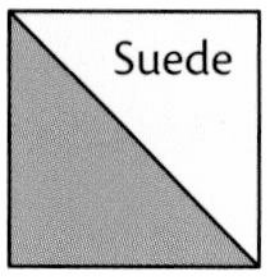

Make 6. 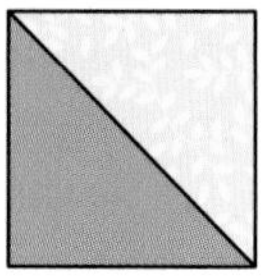   Make 6.

2. Repeat step 1 to make small half-square-triangle units using 2⅞" squares. Layer each of seven red squares with a cream suede square to make 14 units; layer each of 16 red squares with an assorted cream print square to make 32 units;

layer each of five red squares with a green square to make 10 units; layer each of four green squares with a cream faux suede square to make eight units (you'll have one unit left over); layer each of five green squares with an assorted cream print square to make 10 units.

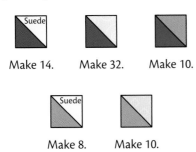

Make 14.   Make 32.   Make 10.

Make 8.   Make 10.

3. Draw a diagonal line from corner to corner on the wrong side of four red 2½" squares. Layer a marked square over each of three small cream suede-and-green half-square-triangle units and one small cream print-and-green half-square-triangle unit so that the drawn line crosses the seam line. Make sure that the cream half of the square is always at the top left when you layer the pieces. Stitch on the drawn lines. Trim ¼" from the stitching line. Press the seam allowances toward the red triangles.

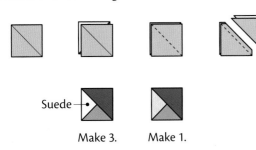

Make 3.   Make 1.

4. To make the large stem squares, draw a diagonal line from corner to corner on the right side of one cream suede 4½" square and two cream print 4½" squares. With right sides together, align the long raw edge of a green 2" x 7" rectangle with the drawn line of each marked square; stitch ½" away from the marked lines. Cut on the drawn lines. Press the seam allowances toward the rectangles. Place the cut-off triangle from each square along the rectangle long raw edge, right sides together, making sure to leave the same amount of the first triangle

exposed on each short edge of the cut-off triangle; sew ½" from the long edges. Press the seam allowances toward the stem and trim the stem ends even with the square.

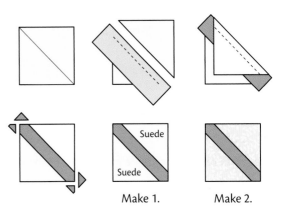

Make 1.   Make 2.

5. Repeat step 4 to make the small stem squares, using six cream suede, six cream print, and four green 2½" squares and the red 1" x 4" rectangles, and sewing ¼" from the marked lines and long edges.

Make 6.   Make 6.   Make 4.

MAKING THE TREE BLOCKS

1. Follow the manufacturer's instructions to apply stabilizer to the wrong side of each yellow, green, and tan faux suede rectangle or square.

2. Cut a random curved line across one long edge of each green and tan rectangle. If you're more comfortable with a drawn line, draw the curve on the stabilizer, and then cut it.

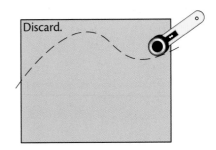

Discard.

3. Layer a green rectangle over each yellow square, aligning the bottom and side straight edges; pin the pieces together. Stitch along the curved line using a decorative stitch and thread to match the green fabric. I used a blanket stitch with the ladders pointing into the green fabric. Be sure to catch the green fabric securely in the stitching. Remove the pins. On the wrong side, trim the excess yellow fabric ¼" from the stitching. Layer a tan curved piece over each green piece, aligning the bottom and side straight edges; pin the pieces together. Stitch the curved line using a decorative stitch and thread to match the tan fabric. I used a blanket stitch with the ladders pointing into the tan fabric. Again, be sure to catch the tan fabric securely in the stitching. Trim the excess green fabric ¼" from the stitching on the wrong side.

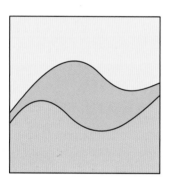

4. Using chalk or a removable marker, draw a 10" square in the center of each background block. Loosely draw the tree outline within each square. Remember, perfection is not required! Using the variegated brown rayon thread, thread paint the trees (see "Drawing Trees with Thread" at right). Tear away the stabilizer when you're finished stitching. Trim the Tree blocks to 12½" x 12½", keeping the design centered.

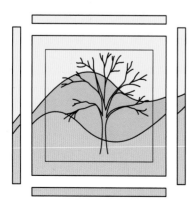

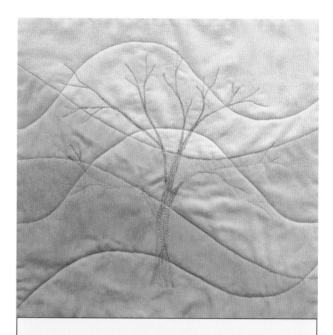

Drawing Trees with Thread

These trees look intimidating to thread paint, but they really are quite fun and easy. Use a free-motion hopping foot or a spring-action darning foot and drop your feed dogs for easier movement of the background fabric. Start at the base of the tree and thread paint up the main center branch by stitching long lines up and down the trunk to build up the width. Angle your main branch off to one side at the top; add smaller branches at the tip and backtrack over the thread a few times to give them dimension. Thread paint three or four more medium branches and add a few small angled branches from these. As you thread paint your tree, remember, branches look more natural in odd-numbered groups.

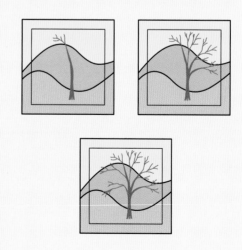

ASSEMBLING THE RUNNER TOP

Lay out the pieced background units, the Tree blocks, and the remaining cream suede, cream print, red, and green squares and rectangles into groups as shown at right. Sew the pieces in each group together, and then sew the groups in each row together. Finally, sew the rows together. Press seam allowances so they oppose each other whenever possible.

FINISHING

If you're making the bed runner reversible, refer to "Runner Flip Side: Rail Fence" (page 93) to make the flip side of the runner before proceeding. If you're not making the bed runner reversible, use the backing fabric in place of the flip side in the following instructions.

1. Refer to "Making the Quilt Sandwich" (page 7) to layer the bed-runner top, batting, and flip side; baste the layers together.

2. Quilt as desired. I stitched in the ditch around each Tree block and then quilted wavy lines within each block. The remainder of the runner was quilted with an allover leaves-and-swirls design to complement both sides. After quilting, trim the batting and flip side even with the runner top.

3. Bind the edges using the tan 2¼"-wide strips and a ¼" seam allowance. Refer to "Binding" (page 7) as needed.

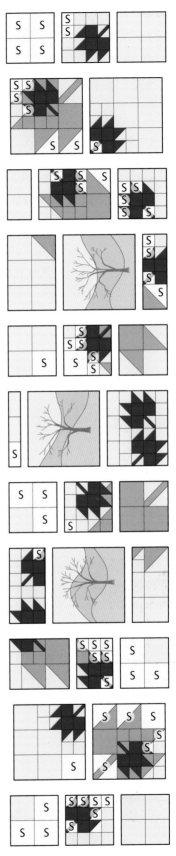

Runner assembly
S = cream faux suede

Just Leaves Shams

Finished Shams: 24½" x 32½"

MATERIALS
(for two standard-size shams)

Yardage is based on 42"-wide fabric unless otherwise noted.

2¼ yards of fabric for flip side

1¼ yards *total* of assorted cream prints for background

¾ yard of cream faux suede for background

⅛ yard of red fabric for leaves

1¾ yard of plain cotton or muslin for front lining

¾ yard of tan fabric for binding

42" x 56" piece of batting

¾ yard of 20"-wide lightweight fusible interfacing

6 same-sized buttons, ⅝" to 1¼" in diameter

CUTTING

From the assorted cream prints, cut a *total* of:
56 squares, 4½" x 4½"
1 square, 2⅞" x 2⅞"
7 squares, 2½" x 2½"

From the cream faux suede fabric, cut:
32 squares, 4½" x 4½"
3 squares, 2⅞" x 2⅞"
11 squares, 2½" x 2½"

From the red fabric, cut:
4 squares, 2⅞" x 2⅞"
6 squares, 2½" x 2½"
2 rectangles, 1" x 4"

From *each* of the lining fabric and batting, cut:
2 rectangles, 28" x 42"

From the flip-side fabric, cut:
2 rectangles, 24½" x 25½"
2 rectangles, 24½" x 14½"

From the interfacing, cut:
2 strips, 1½" x 24½"

From the tan fabric, cut:
7 strips, 3⅛" x 42"

MAKING THE SHAMS

1. Refer to "Making Half-Square-Triangle Units" (page 5) to layer each of three red 2⅞" squares with a cream faux suede 2⅞" square to make six half-square-triangle units. Repeat with one red 2⅞" square and the assorted cream print 2⅞" square to make two units.

2. Using one cream faux suede 2½" square, one cream print 2½" square, and the two red 1" x 4" rectangles, refer to step 4 of "Making the Background Units" (page 86) to make two stem units.

3. Lay out the pieced units and remaining squares and rectangles into vertical rows, following the sham assembly diagrams (page 91). Sew the 2½" squares and half-square-triangle units in the

third and fourth rows together first, and then continue to assemble each row. Press the seam allowances in opposite directions from row to row. Sew the rows together. Press the seam allowances in one direction.

Sham assembly
S = cream faux suede

4. Refer to "Making the Quilt Sandwich" (page 7) to layer each sham top with backing and batting; baste the layers together. Quilt as desired. I used the same leaf-and-swirls design that I used on the runner.

5. Refer to "Making the Sham" (page 15) to make the sham flip-side pieces, applying the interfacing to the 24½"-long edges. Stitch the fronts and flip-side pieces together, following "The Still Easy but Reversible Sham" instructions. Bind the edges of each sham using the tan 3⅛"-wide strips and a ½" seam allowance. Stitch 2" from the edges of each sham to make the flange. Sew the buttons to the button bands to correspond to the buttonholes.

One More Leaf Pillow

Finished Pillow: 20" x 20"

MATERIALS

Yardage is based on 42"-wide fabric unless otherwise noted.

⅔ yard of fabric for flip side

¼ yard of cream faux suede fabric for inner border

¼ yard *total* of assorted cream prints for Leaf block

¼ yard of green fabric for Leaf block

¼ yard of red fabric for outer border

22" x 22" piece of plain cotton or muslin for front backing

22" x 22" piece of batting

⅔ yard of 20"-wide lightweight fusible interfacing

2 yards of 2"-wide fringe

3 same-size buttons, ⅝" to 1¼" in diameter

20" x 20" pillow form

CUTTING

From the cream faux suede, cut:

2 strips, 2½" x 12½"

2 strips, 2½" x 16½"

From the assorted cream prints, cut a *total* of:

2 squares, 4⅞" x 4⅞"

2 squares, 4½" x 4½"

From the green fabric, cut:

2 squares, 4⅞" x 4⅞"

3 squares, 4½" x 4½"

1 rectangle, 2" x 7"

From the red fabric, cut:

2 strips, 2¾" x 21"

2 strips, 2¾" x 16½"

From the flip-side fabric, cut:

1 rectangle, 16½" x 21"

1 rectangle, 12" x 21"

From the interfacing, cut:

2 strips, 1½" x 21"

MAKING THE PILLOW

1. Refer to "Making Half-Square-Triangle Units" (page 5) to layer a cream print 4⅞" square over each of the green 4⅞" squares to make four half-square-triangle units.

2. Using one cream print 4½" square and the green 2" x 7" rectangle, refer to step 4 of "Making the Background Units" (page 86) to make one stem unit.

3. Refer to the pillow assembly diagram at right to lay out the half-square-triangle units, stem unit, and green and cream 4½" squares in three vertical rows. Sew the pieces in each row together. Press the seam allowances in opposite directions from row to row. Sew the rows together. Press the seam allowances toward the center row.

4. Sew the cream suede 2½" x 12½" inner-border strips to the sides of the Leaf block. Press the seam allowances toward the border strips. Add the cream suede 2½" x 16½" strips to the top and bottom of the block. Press the seam allowances toward the border strips. Repeat with the red strips, sewing the shorter strips to the sides and the longer strips to the top and bottom.

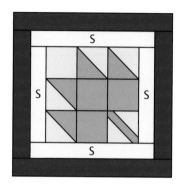

Pillow assembly
S = cream faux suede

FINISHING

1. Refer to "Making the Quilt Sandwich" (page 7) to layer the backing, batting, and pillow top; baste the layers together. Stitch in the ditch of the block and border seams.

2. Align the lip edge of the fringe with the raw edges of the pillow front and sew it in place.

3. Refer to "Making the Flip Side" (page 14) to make the flip-side pieces. They will not be backed or quilted.

4. Refer to "Assembling the Pillow" (page 14) to finish the pillow, being careful not to catch the fringe in the seam.

Runner Flip Side: Rail Fence

Unfinished Runner: 30" x 114" • Finished Block: 5¾" x 5¾"

MATERIALS

Yardage is based on 42"-wide fabric. Binding, backing, and batting yardages are given with the "Leaves-and-Trees Runner" materials list on page 86.

⅜ yard *each* of light, medium, and dark fabrics in red, green, gold, and blue

⅝ yard of brown fabric

CUTTING

From *each* of the 4 light, 4 medium, and 4 dark fabrics, cut:

4 strips, 2½" x 42" (48 total)

From the brown fabric, cut:

13 squares, 6½" x 6½"

MAKING THE RAIL FENCE BLOCKS

Sew a light, medium, and dark red strip together along the long edges in order from light to dark to make a strip set. Make a *total* of four red strip sets. Repeat with the green, gold, and blue strips. Crosscut the red, green, and gold strip sets *each* into 20 blocks, 6½" wide. Crosscut the blue strip sets into 22 blocks, 6½".

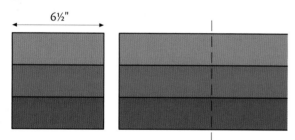

Make 4 strip sets each of red, green, gold, and blue.
Cut 20 blocks each of red, green, and gold.
Cut 22 blue blocks.

ASSEMBLING AND FINISHING

1. Lay out the blocks and brown 6½" squares in horizontal rows as shown, making sure the pieced blocks are rotated properly. Sew the pieces in each row together. Press the seam allowances in opposite directions from row to row. Sew the rows together. Press the seam allowances in one direction.

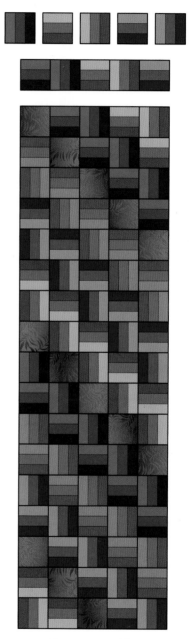

Runner assembly

2. Refer to the finishing instructions for "Leaves and Trees Runner" (page 89) to layer, quilt, and bind the runner.